KINGFISHERS
& KOOKABURRAS

KINGFISHERS
& KOOKABURRAS

DAVID HOLLANDS

Jewels of the Australian Bush

Reed New Holland

First published in Australia in 1999 by
Reed New Holland
an imprint of New Holland Publishers (Australia) Pty Ltd
Sydney • Auckland • London • Cape Town

14 Aquatic Drive, Frenchs Forest NSW 2086, Australia
218 Lake Road, Northcote Auckland, New Zealand
24 Nutford Place, London W1H 6DQ, United Kingdom
80 McKenzie Street, Cape Town 8001, South Africa

National Library of Australia Cataloguing-in-Publication Data:

Hollands, David, 1933–
Kingfishers and Kookaburras: Jewels of the Australian bush

Bibliography.
Includes index.
ISBN 1 876334 32 0

1. Kingfishers - Australia. 2. Kookaburra. I. Title.

598.78

Publishing General Manager: Jane Hazell
Publisher: Averill Chase
Project Manager: Fiona Doig
Editor: Emma Wise
Consultant: Ken Simpson
Designer: Jo Waite Design
Cartographer: John Hall (main map); Jo Waite, distribution maps
Reproduction: DNL Resources
Printer: Kyodo Printing, Singapore

Captions
Acknowledgments (page vii): Blue-winged Kookaburra (left);
Yellow-billed Kingfisher (right).
Foreword (page ix): Azure Kingfisher (left); Sacred Kingfisher (right).
Contents (page xi): Laughing Kookaburra (left); Forest Kingfisher (right).
Introduction (page 1): Little Kingfisher (left); Collared Kingfisher (right).
References (page 128): Azure Kingfisher (left); Yellow-billed Kingfisher (right).
Index (page 130): Red-backed Kingfisher (left); Buff-breasted Paradise-
Kingfisher (right).

For Margaret

ACKNOWLEDGMENTS

The help of some very good friends has not only eased the task of writing this book but also made it immensely more pleasurable. At the top of the list are John and Junell Young. John has been a pillar of strength to me for many years now and he once again excelled himself. He is a man who will never admit defeat and regards any temporary setback merely as a springboard from which to launch the next attempt. We travelled widely through Queensland on this venture but many of the birds lived close to his home and Junell always welcomed me and treated me as one of the family.

In Queensland I had many helpers. Russell and Christine Kirkwood, Jack and May Hobbs and the late Bob Allingham with his wife Marge all gave me complete access to their farms and I was given similar privileges by the Queensland Forestry Department in Ingham. Ray Venables put in a lot of time trying to find the Little Kingfisher as did Chris and Denise Dahlberg of Daintree. Jim Browning did all the groundwork for the Collared Kingfisher, which made the study itself quite easy.

In Victoria a long list of sharp-eyed spies have spotted birds or nests: Ray and Lynn Brown, Peter Coulton, John, Ginger and Helen Johnstone, Roddy Kleinitz, Merv Morris, Charlie Owen, Alan and Susan Robertson, Norman Webb and John Woodgate. Peter May and Steve De Voogd helped me with constructing observation towers, Howard and Jill Plowright with Azure Kingfishers and Alan Cook went to great trouble to make me a special tank to attempt pictures of birds under water.

When I asked Peter O'Reilly to write a foreword, he accepted at once and I thank him for doing so and for giving it such generous treatment. I am also extremely grateful to Ken Simpson, who reviewed the manuscript, made numerous additions to the bibliography and significantly reworked the distribution maps.

My whole family is always supportive of my obsessions but I particularly thank my daughter Louise who works for Qantas and has helped organise much of my travels.

Finally, there is my wife Margaret. Not only has she has come on expeditions, sat in hides and waded through cold rivers to catch little fish, she has also put up cheerfully with my frequent absences, done more than her share in the medical practice and been both spur and critic in a project which, at times, seemed likely to go on for ever. I dedicate this book to her.

FOREWORD

The world of birds has a magical appeal. They can capture us and hold us enthralled for a lifetime. How else could David Hollands find the enthusiasm and the time to escape his busy medical practice to track down and photograph every kingfisher species in Australia?

Wildlife photography is a waiting game and photographers have a great opportunity to observe and record the habits of their subjects. David has not wasted his time behind the camera. He has introduced us to each bird in a most personal way, highlighting its unique traits and individual personality. His vision of a shady stream and the jewel-like Azure Kingfisher invites you to go there and be a part of it yourself. The emotions that surface remind me of Wordsworth's response when observing, of all things, a nesting sparrow.

> *She gave me eyes, she gave me ears,*
> *And humble cares and delicate fears,*
> *A heart, the fountain of sweet tears,*
> *And love and thought and joy.*

I believe that David's book, with its excellent text and photography, gives people the eyes and ears to see and hear a world that perhaps they never knew existed. Thanks, David, for leading us with your camera and your pen to some wild and exotic places: to those secluded nest sites that are the home of the Kingfishers.

Peter O' Reilly.

Green Mountains, Canungra, Queensland

CONTENTS

INTRODUCTION

Kingfishers and kookaburras! They are strong contenders for the title of "most spectacular group" of all Australian birds: vibrant in colour, conspicuous in activity and, in many species, inescapably strident in voice. I have heard them described as jewels of the Australian bush and it seems a wonderfully apt name for this dramatically sparkling family. This book is a celebration of those jewels and my main aim is to show them in that light.

There are, at the latest count, 90 species of kingfisher in the world and Australia has 10 of them (two endemics and eight that we share). They inhabit every continent, except Antarctica, and occur in a huge variety of sizes, colours, habitats and adaptations for living.

They range in size from the tiny, 10-gram African Pygmy Kingfisher to the Giant Kingfisher of Africa and the Laughing Kookaburra of Australia, both of which may weigh close to half a kilogram. Their colours range across the whole spectrum, with blue a recurring feature in a majority of species and only the Pied Kingfisher of Africa being restricted to a simple, but still very striking, black and white. They have adapted to rivers and deserts, to wet rainforests and dry woodlands, to mangrove swamps and tiny offshore islands. They have learned to catch lizards, snakes and spiders on the ground, to dive underwater for fish, to snatch frogs in the tree canopy and take insects in full flight. Some take young birds from their nests and others find food by shovelling deeply in the ground. They are, indeed, a versatile group.

Taxonomists believe that kingfishers had their origins in the forests of South-East Asia and northern Australasia. From there they radiated in all directions so it is now possible to see kingfishers in places as disparate as the waters of the Amazon, the lakes of Alaska, the dry thornbush of southern Africa and many of the remote islands of the South Pacific. Nevertheless, South-East Asia and Australia continue to be the world's kingfisher centres and it is in this region that the greatest number of species occur.

For all their diversity, kingfishers retain a number of characteristic features that make them readily recognizable to anyone with even a passing knowledge of birds. The oversize bill, top-heavy bearing, tubby body, short tail and, in many species, iridescent blue of at least some feathers all combine to form a shape that can only be a kingfisher. Many non-birding people have remarked to me that the kookaburra looks just like a big kingfisher, unwittingly spotting the characteristics that make the group unique.

The Sacred Kingfisher.

In a book on kingfishers, pictures must be more important than words and I have taken this approach. Most kingfishers require flight or bright sunlight to be seen at their best and I have concentrated on this, trying to find some moment when I could freeze a bird in midair. The essays are drawn from my own observations in the field and although in such a close-knit group there are some inevitable similarities, it is remarkable how different a story could be told for each bird. This is not a textbook but there are some who may want to use it for reference and I have included a field guide section too. Inevitably, that section contains some information that is outside my own experience and I have drawn heavily here on other works of reference.

Jewels of the Australian bush! Above all, this is a celebration of those jewels, a book for those who have already thrilled to the sight of a kingfisher as well as for those who have yet to do so.

CHAPTER ONE
AZURE KINGFISHER

"Mountains without eagles are only landscape!" So said Wolfgang Baumgart, one of the world's great raptor experts. I have never forgotten his words for they speak so aptly both of the wildness of nature and of the needs of the human spirit.

This is not the only pairing that needs to be made before the two become complete. Rivers and kingfishers! A stream may seem lovely in its own right but let a kingfisher appear and it comes to life, shimmering with the light and colour of this living jewel.

There are around 90 species of kingfisher in the world and it may come as a surprise to learn that only a third are birds of lakes and rivers. The remainder are dry-land kingfishers, not dependent on water for their hunting and nesting, even though some may still occasionally dive for prey.

It is the electric-blue River Kingfisher of Europe that is so familiar and is responsible for the group's popular association with water. So well known is it that it was long called *the* Kingfisher, a title that ignored the existence of the many other species, some of which are very closely related. One of these is the Azure Kingfisher of Australia, similar in shape, size and behaviour to the River Kingfisher but an even deeper and richer blue in colour. I hesitate to call it Australia's most beautiful kingfisher – almost every species seems to deserve that title when seen at close quarters – but there is certainly none that surpasses it. The upperparts are a deep shimmering blue contrasting with the chestnut breast and belly. There is a slash of white on the sides of the neck, the long dagger bill is black and shiny and the tiny legs and feet are bright red. Like many kingfishers, it takes sunlight to bring out the colours and, perched in the shade or on a dull day, the Azure can appear quite drab or even black.

Along the waterways of eastern and northern Australia, the Azure Kingfisher is not a rare bird but, despite its colour, it can be remarkably cryptic and difficult to spot. It tends to choose shady perches and, for many people, their first sight of it is a streak of blue, disturbed by their approaching boat, or a rare view of one perched in the open on the rails of a jetty.

I started looking for Azure Kingfishers in 1992, thinking that it would be a relatively easy task. It was not. Instead it has taken me until 1998 to achieve anything like the coverage that I had planned. The reasons for this are many. Not every waterway has kingfishers. Human disturbance, pollution, lack of nest sites and too-rapid flow can all make a river unsuitable for kingfishers. Thickets of

On the Brodribb River, an Azure Kingfisher perches with its catch. This very brightly coloured bird is a male.

blackberries or lantana make some streams impossible to approach while others have channels where alternating snags and waterholes are a barrier to human progress, either by boat or on foot. Then there are the problems of predation, erratic breeding seasons, inaccessible nest sites and, not least, the kingfisher's ability to conceal the whereabouts of its nest hole. The challenge was much greater than I could ever have anticipated.

One Azure Kingfisher characteristic that makes study a bit simpler is their habitual use of favoured sites and perches for fishing. This may be for just a few days or weeks at an ephemeral pool but there is a little creek near my home in Victoria where I have been watching kingfishers hunting from the same dead stick for over five years.

I have watched kingfishers along a creek in north Queensland that I know well. For much of the year it is a creek in name only, a dry channel punctuated by the occasional muddy waterhole. Where the kingfishers go at such times, I have never discovered but, with the coming of the wet season, they are back, reclaiming old territories and raising their young.

In the moment before touchdown, the Azure Kingfisher shows off the dazzling blue of its plumage.

In mid-February 1993 the wet season was well established and, after weeks of rain, the creek was in full spate. Below a low waterfall the river ran white and foaming. This created perfect conditions for little fish and the kingfishers hunted here every day. My hide was close to the water's edge, not particularly camouflaged, but kingfishers seem not to worry too much about new structures provided they cannot detect movement.

I heard him coming some distance away, a shrill whistle, so high as to be almost above human hearing. Moments later he was in sight, a streak of cobalt just above the water, wings moving so fast they were just a blur. He came to the waterfall, lifted to clear its broken surface and sped on, as transient as a flash of lightning, gone so quickly that he became reality and memory at almost the same moment. Ten minutes later he shot past again, back downstream, then upstream again and back, passing at such speed I could not make out if he had prey or not. I began to wonder if I had my hide in the wrong place but then the whistle came again and suddenly he was there, perched on a dry paperbark twig three metres above the water and peering down intently.

Kingfishers don't waste time when they see prey. After only moments he dropped off the perch in a slanting dive, hitting the water immediately below the falls. How he could see down into that turbulence is a mystery but he emerged with a struggling fish and took it away at once, flying downstream and out of sight round a bend.

With his first dive successful, he returned, this time perching in the open and much closer to me. Clearly there were plenty of fish but the broken water must have made it difficult. The next two

Arriving with a fish, the adult's beak is into the nest hole before its feet have landed.

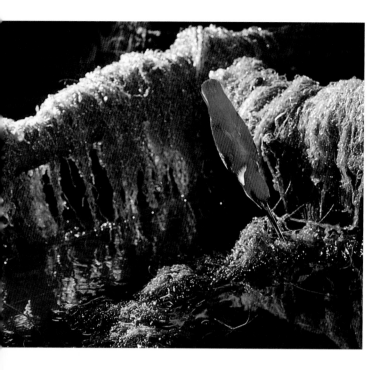

The Fisherman. Top left: At the start of the dive, the kingfisher becomes an arrow with wings drawn in tightly against the body. Top right: Nearing the water, the wings begin to open to control the depth of the dive. Above Left: Impact! Amid the splash of its entry, the wingtips just show above the water. Above Right: In a shower of spray, the kingfisher emerges from the creek. Opposite: It flies off with a fish held firmly in its bill.

Azure Kingfisher

dives were unproductive but he returned each time to the same vantage point. He dived again – a splash, a cloud of spray and he was back on his way downstream with another little fish.

While kingfishers do have a dagger-shaped bill, it is used not as a dagger but rather as a pair of pincers. There is no stab wound in the prey caught and the bird always comes up from the water with the fish held crossways, only later shifting it head inwards for swallowing or head outwards for feeding young. How they manage to catch fish at all is a source of wonder to me. Refraction, distance, turbulence, discoloured water and fish movement are only some of the factors the birds have to overcome, but the success rate of their hunting dives is remarkably high.

I stayed in the hide for some hours and, late in the afternoon, a second kingfisher appeared and was fed by the first one. Perhaps this was courtship feeding by the male but so late in the breeding season it seemed more likely that he was caring for a newly fledged young bird. The next day, this became virtually certain when he flew past with a fish, pursued by two other kingfishers.

Eight months later I returned to the same spot only to face a very different scene. Wet season had given place to dry, the creek had long ceased running and was reduced to a few muddy pools. Despite their appearance, however, these were not stagnant. Beneath the surface, water continued to flow through the sands and, surprisingly, there were still fish there. Kingfishers were also still about and, at one tiny waterhole, only three metres across, they came every day, perching among the roots of a fallen tree and hunting with great success. In the driest of years even these last fishing spots disappear and nobody knows where the birds go then but, when the creek starts running again, they invariably return as they do along a host of similar creeks throughout tropical Australia.

In 1994 I tried to photograph at a nest along this creek. Azure Kingfishers always nest in banks, usually over water, although in the tropics they sometimes choose dry gullies, possibly as an insurance against sudden flooding. This pair had made their hole high on the bank of the creek, safe from all but the biggest floods. However, flooding is not the only form danger can take.

On 22 February there were large young in the nest, a few days short of flying. I returned two days later to build the hide. One kingfisher was there but seemed agitated and we sensed that all was not well. I shone a torch down the hole and the light reflected back off the head of a Brown Snake, lying just inside the tunnel. It had already eaten the young and may even have taken an adult, too, for we could see only one. Predation takes a huge toll on nesting birds everywhere but it seems particularly severe in the tropics where the wastage rate for all species is enormous.

For two more seasons, I followed the Azures in north Queensland, learning much about them but being frustrated by many failures. At some nests, the young flew before we could find them, several nests were abandoned for no obvious cause, another one was robbed by a snake and there were several that were unsuited to photography. I turned my attentions to Victoria and to kingfishers that lived closer to home.

The flood plain of the Snowy and Brodribb rivers covers about 150 square kilometres around Orbost. It is a complex area, a patchwork of farmland, swamp and estuary, criss-crossed with numerous creeks and artificial channels. Azure Kingfishers are common here but it is not easy country to search. Both rivers have changed their courses many times, leaving a confusion of pools, billabongs and narrow drainage channels. It took a long time to begin to unravel their secrets.

The Milly is one such channel, running into the Brodribb River. From the main river, its entrance is almost invisible, obscured by overhanging foliage and only wide enough for a canoe. Open cow pastures are just a few hundred metres away but, in the dim light along the channel, there is the feeling of being in some primeval place. Dense tea-trees arch overhead, shutting out the sky. The trees are clothed in luxuriant moss and the air is still and heavy with the smell of decaying vegetation.

Unseen until it flew, a kingfisher emerged from the thicket and flickered along the channel to perch on a low branch. The boat moved on, gliding slowly against the ebbing tide and the

Scattering sand, an Azure Kingfisher drops away from its nest hole on the Snowy River.

kingfisher moved with it, changing perches just often enough to stay a safe distance in front. In most places the banks were low and went under water at high tide but there were two spots where there was still a metre or two of vertical bank when the tide was full. Both of these bore several of the characteristic circular entrances to old kingfisher burrows. It was July, midwinter and far outside the breeding season but the birds were still here and the signs were good.

I returned in mid-October. Azure Kingfishers are late breeders in Victoria, not usually starting until late spring, and this visit was meant purely as a reconnaissance. It looked promising from the start. The first bank revealed the entrances to two new holes. There was no sign of a bird, however, and possibly these holes had been started and then abandoned. Kingfishers make straight tunnels and must start again if they strike a rock or a tree root.

A little farther upstream lay the second bank, lower than the first and at no point more than a metre above high tide. Halfway up was a fresh hole. I had only just spotted it when a kingfisher catapulted itself out of the entrance and away up the channel. It looked like a female and she came out head first, a sure sign that the egg chamber was complete for only there does the bird have room to turn around. I quietly reversed the boat and eased away. It was very early in the season and any interference with the nest could easily cause a desertion.

The Azure Kingfisher's head becomes a blur as it beats its prey against a branch.

It was 27 October, over a fortnight later, before I had a chance to return. By this time the eggs should have hatched but, after my Queensland experiences, I was a bit apprehensive, particularly when the bird failed to fly from the hole. I shone the torch, half expecting to see the head of yet another snake. There was no snake and, at the end of the long tunnel, I could just make out the young, not newly hatched as I had expected but coloured, feathered and nearly ready to fly. I had totally miscalculated the dates and these babies would have been nine or 10 days old at the time of my first visit.

I had intended to do a detailed study at this nest but there was no time for that and I had to be content with two short sessions from a camouflaged hide across the channel. The light was poor and the water muddy but this was no handicap to the kingfishers, which came four times with fish during both my visits. Usually the fish were held lengthways in the bill with the head facing forwards for easy presentation to the chicks. However, one huge fish was nearly half the length of the bird, far too long to be carried within the bill, and was held crossways with head and tail drooping either side of the kingfisher's bill like some grotesque moustache.

That seemed likely to mark the end of Azure Kingfishers for 1996 but, within days of the young flying, I heard of another nest, a much easier one to approach where I would not need a boat. It was 17 November, nearly three weeks since the other brood had fledged. I knew nothing of the constancy of the Azure breeding season and wondered if I would be too late.

My fears were unfounded. As I climbed down the bank, I could hear the rhythmic swizzling calls of young kingfishers. They went quiet when I shone the torch into the hole and I could make out five of them. They were still small, looking distinctly reptilian in the leaden blue quills from which the feathers would soon burst. I estimated that the chicks were about 10 days old.

Set among the roots of Lightwood and Willow and well above even the highest of king tides, this was, for my purpose, a much better site than the last one. There was a sand ledge big enough for a small hide and ample anchorage points for equipment.

Azure Kingfishers may conceal their nests well but they are not shy and, after two days, I was ready to start. By this time there was a considerable array of tripods, clamps and flashes around the entrance but there was no sign of hesitation as the birds came in to the nest. It took a few minutes to organise myself in the hide and, by the time I was ready, both kingfishers were waiting impatiently, perched on dead sticks in the river, each with a fish in its bill. From the mouth of the tunnel came the incessant sounds of the young.

The male came in first. His brighter colours distinguished him from his mate and he was consistently the bolder of the two. He flew straight up to the hole, landed on the lip and went inside, all in one movement. The tunnel was nearly 50 centimetres long and I never saw the young come forward to be fed, even when they were within a day or two of flying. He was inside for little more than 10 seconds, reversing out and hurling himself away from the bank to twist round in flight and skim away across the river.

Close to the far bank a dead stick poked from the river and he stopped there, perching for a few moments before plunging into the water and back to the stick. He did it twice more before flying on, a pattern of behaviour I have noticed with almost every pair of nesting Azures I have ever watched. Usually they use a perch but sometimes it is a headlong plunge while in full flight across the water. After squeezing backwards out of a hole full of loose dirt and faeces, the need for a bath is not hard to understand.

At earlier nests I had watched, feeding usually occurred about two or three times an hour but here the rate was extraordinary. At one stage on that first day the birds made seven visits in 10 minutes and 11 in 20, each time bringing food. Well over half the prey was fish but there were also numbers of small black crustaceans, which appeared to be a type of crayfish. At this early stage, all of the fish I saw were small and could be carried easily within a kingfisher's bill. Later on, when the young were bigger, some of the fish were enormous and over half the length of the kingfisher that had caught them. David Boag, who watched kingfishers in England, made similar observations and I have no doubt that the adults choose the size of their prey to suit that of their young.

The ability of the young kingfishers to consume food was astonishing. Most of my sessions were in the mornings and it was unusual for the adults to come less than four times an hour. Even allowing for fewer visits in the afternoon, this represents a daily catch of some 50 fish or nearly 1500

Still water. A creek typical of the kind favoured by the Azure Kingfisher in eastern Victoria.

Below the waterfall. An Azure Kingfisher watches for the movement of a fish.

during the fledging period, taking no account of the fish the adults kept for themselves. I have not weighed any fish of similar size but, at 10 each per day, the young kingfishers must surely go close to eating their own weight in fish every day.

They flew on 5 December at an age of between 26 and 30 days. The next morning I was unable to find them but there are trees down to the water all along this river and I did not have time to look very far. For several days before this, they had looked ready to go, immaculate in their new blue plumage but still with the shorter bills that would distinguish them from their parents for some time.

Now I felt my Azure season really had ended. It was high summer and few birds of any sort nest in Victoria at this time. I don't know quite what prompted me to have a last look but I went back on 24 January, six weeks and one day after the young had flown. I was greeted by the sight of an obviously well-used burrow with the familiar calls of young kingfishers issuing from it. Not only were there three baby kingfishers inside but they looked to be at least two weeks old.

Allowing three weeks for incubation, this put laying at only a week after the previous brood had flown, a most unexpected finding. It meant that the adults may still have been finding food for their first brood while incubating eggs for the second. Of course, I had no guarantee that the first brood had survived but it seems unlikely that all five would have perished. Perhaps the young can fish for themselves within a few days of fledging but that also seems unlikely. Certainly, that unexpected finding raised some intriguing questions and, so far, I do not have the answers.

Near the kingfishers' nest lived a number of the aquatic Eastern Water Dragons. The biggest one, fully a metre in length, often used a hole in the bank almost beside the kingfishers' hole. Mindful of the monitor lizard's predilection for digging out the mounds of other kingfishers, I was fearful that the same would happen here but the Azures seemed quite unconcerned by the water dragons' presence and the nest was left undisturbed.

The young left on 8 February and I suspect that fledging took a little longer than with the first brood. Certainly, when I was in the hide, the feeding visits were less frequent. Possibly fish were scarcer but maybe the adults were still having to supply both broods.

I had intended that to be my last Azure Kingfisher nest but, when another opportunity presents, it is hard to resist the temptation to become involved again. It seemed to be a particularly good year for Azures in 1997 and I knew of four active nests within easy reach of home. The pair on the Snowy River had young in the nest by mid-November. The hole was in a vertical sandy bank on the outside of a bend in the river. The sand was soft and free of vegetation, an excellent site for the kingfishers, but the river was swinging ever wider here and the bank looked decidedly unstable.

I visited the bank several times in late November, listening for the whistle of the returning adults and watching them come in low to their approach perch just above the water. Once there they would wait, taking stock and making sure that all was well before whirring up to the hole in an ever-steepening climb so that the the final approach was almost vertical with the bird tight in to the bank.

I was then away for 10 days and it was the start of the second week in December before I could return. At first it seemed that all was well, but then I realised that the birds were behaving strangely. Both adults were there: the male with a fish, the female without. Repeatedly the female flew to the hole and went inside for up to three minutes. As she emerged, she kicked out copious amounts of fine grey soil, which fell and lay conspicuously on the yellow sand below. Then the male went in with his fish but stayed only a few moments before coming out, still with the fish. He did this twice before flying to a perch and swallowing the fish himself. I left, puzzled, with the female still flying to the hole and digging.

Waiting in the shadows, a favourite spot for the Azure Kingfisher.

Another capture. Small fish are held within the bill but large ones like this are held diagonally or crosswise.

It was another week before I was able to go back. There had been rain and I returned to find that the bank had collapsed. I had earlier measured the length of the tunnel at 61 centimetres but most of it had now gone and only the innermost 15 centimetres remained. There was no sign of the chicks and I had no means of telling if they had escaped burial. It seemed unlikely and, with hindsight, I felt sure the slip had already begun the previous week with the female trying to dig her way back into a tunnel that was already partly obliterated.

I wondered if the kingfishers would dig the hole out again. They didn't, but the speed with which they made alternative arrangements caught me completely by surprise. I went back on 16 December, six days after I had found the collapse. There was no sign of fresh digging at the old site but then I noticed a new hole, four metres downstream from the first one and close to the top of the bank. It had not been there the previous week but, when I gently probed it, my stick went in for 67 centimetres, an astonishing week's work for a little bird with no tools but its beak and a pair of puny feet.

I followed the fortunes of this nest until the beginning of February and hope the young got away safely. It was hard to be certain. A nearby irrigation pump clattered away by day and night, making it impossible to hear the young and, with the river level at a record low, the adults were having difficulty finding enough fish. On the days I watched there was usually at least an hour between visits, a far cry from the 11 in 20 minutes I had witnessed on the Brodribb River the previous year.

This tunnel was too long to be able to see the young with a torch but, on 13 February, there were some wisps of spider's web in the tunnel, firm proof that the birds were no longer visiting. That was seven weeks and five days since they had finished the new tunnel, just about long enough to complete a successful breeding cycle if the eggs were layed as soon as digging was finished. I never spotted any fledged young so the truth will remain a mystery.

The more I saw of the Azure Kingfisher, the more fascinated I became. Their amazing fishing powers were particularly intriguing and I was determined to record this on film. With most kingfishers hunting over several kilometres of creek, this seemed likely to be a somewhat difficult process. The alternative was to persuade the kingfisher to hunt at a place of my choosing.

I selected a spot along a narrow creek where the birds had a favourite fishing perch. The first task was to create a small pool within the creek that water could flow through but where small fish could be contained. By keeping the pool stocked with fish, I hoped to persuade the kingfishers to hunt there. Once this had happened, I could introduce cameras, flashes and infra-red beams and, if these were accepted, begin photography.

It might sound quite straightforward but theory and practice are rarely the same and the way forward was strewn with problems, both the expected and the totally unpredictable. The creek was tidal, only by a few centimetres but enough to make the difference between fish that were captive and fish that could make good their escape. Even catching the fish was a much greater problem than I had anticipated. Baited fish traps produced a paltry few and I found the only reliable method was to use a 20-metre net in the river estuary, wading in neck-deep and dragging the net while my wife Margaret walked with the other end along the water's edge. In midwinter it was a chilling experience. It had to be repeated several times a week, but at least it worked.

Once they had found the fish, the birds seemed quite happy to come and catch them, regardless of what I put round their pond. Tripods, cameras, flashes and light beams were all accepted readily and, when I found a kingfisher sitting on top of a tripod in preference to its natural perch, I knew that all shyness had been overcome. The problems of lighting and of exactly where to site the infrared beam were not easy but that was nothing new. Eventually all was ready.

There are no certainties in wildlife photography and here there were more uncertainties than usual. All the equipment was perilously close to the salt water and was unprotected against rain. The numerous batteries had to last all day and the critical alignment of the beam had to remain undisturbed. Most vital of all, the kingfisher must follow my anticipated dive path.

At the end of the first day I returned to find that the camera had gone off twice. The following day, there were four exposures. It wasn't much but it was a start. However, when the processed film came back, the bird was too small in the frame and the lighting needed some correction.

I made the adjustments and tried again. Coming back at the end of the day, I was amazed to find that I had a complete roll of 36 exposures. Clearly everything was working superbly and I was back the next morning to set up again. Once more, I found myself with a completely exposed roll of film and, with keen anticipation, dispatched them for processing.

I have learned to take nothing for granted in wildlife photography but I was quite unprepared for the results that came back. There were no kingfisher pictures at all but I had 72 shots of various segments of a White-faced Heron's anatomy: a foot, a head, a beak, a part of the back or a section of the breast. It was not only kingfishers that could make use of my supply of fish.

The creek flooded and I had some equipment failures but the technique did work. Amazingly, the White-faced Heron never returned and, in time, I found myself with a collection of highly revealing pictures. In the full dive the kingfisher becomes a dart, a straight line from beak to tail, body so stretched and taut that the bird appears wingless. In a deep dive it enters the water like this but to take fish nearer the surface it goes in with wings half open, a technique that permits it to dive safely and effectively in the shallowest of creeks. The stubby wings allow the bird literally to fly under water and explode vertically upwards at the end of the dive. The sleek feathers are completely water-repellent and, leaving the water, the bird is as dry as when it went in. Now it remains to photograph kingfishers underwater, a challenge that has so far defeated me.

CHAPTER TWO
LITTLE KINGFISHER

I had always expected the Little Kingfisher to be tiny but even so the first meeting came as something of a surprise. Many kingfishers are on the small side, among them the Azure, which I knew well, but the Little Kingfisher is in a different class altogether.

The setting was a rainforest stream in north Queensland, scarcely a stride across, an anabranch of the main creek. It was dark there, the light closed off by the forest canopy arching above it. Along the watercourse were pools, not very big but deep enough to hold a population of little fish.

I heard it first, a shrill, thin, whistle, very similar to the Azure Kingfisher but even weaker and higher so that it was almost above human hearing. Then I saw it, flying directly towards me and so small that, for a moment, I thought I was looking at a large insect. In the gloom, the blue of its plumage might as well have been black and it was the patches of white beside the bill that stood out, twin headlights to mark its flight along the creek. Only when it came alongside me did the true colours show, bright blue above and clean white below.

It landed, seemingly unconcerned by my presence, barely 20 metres away. The perch it chose was a flimsy dead twig, little thicker than a leaf stem. So light was the kingfisher that the twig barely quivered. After a while, a dragonfly came and landed below it. The wingspan of the dragonfly was close to twice the length of the kingfisher.

The bird was hunting, peering into the rippled water for sight of a fish. It bobbed its head, gauging its aim, and then dived: a quick, shallow plunge that at once allowed for distance, refraction and the dark-coloured water. It was all over in a flash and a tiny fish struggled in the pincer grip of the kingfisher's bill. It flew back to the twig, swallowed the fish and was away, leaving the creek to be lost at once in the forest.

That was 1992 and the start of my involvement with Little Kingfishers. Since then, I have seen many more but my main goal has been to find an active nest and, six years on, that goal still eludes me. The bird books give holes in trees and river banks as the Little Kingfisher's nesting sites. The former is certainly true but, in north Queensland at least, I am doubtful if holes in banks are used.

The tiny Little Kingfisher is the second-smallest kingfisher in the world.

At first it looked as though the search would be quite easy. Along that tiny creek we found at least one bird almost every visit. Being so small, they were quite hard to spot and the best tactic was to wait and let the bird reveal itself, its shrill whistle followed by the tiny, darting form.

After a while it became clear there were two birds and, by January, they were often at the same spot along the creek, close to a thin, rotten tree stump. Then they started to excavate, digging out a tiny circular hole in the pulpy wood. The birds worked rapidly. Within a few days, the cavity was large enough for one bird to disappear inside. Soon afterwards, they had room enough to turn round again and come out head first.

Throughout this time, the pair bond was becoming stronger and stronger. Oblivious to human presence, they perched side-by-side close to the nest hole, copulating frequently between bouts of digging. When the female began to spend long periods inside, there seemed little doubt that laying had started. Then it was all over. Whether a predator found the nest or one of the birds was killed, I shall never know but, one day, the kingfishers were gone and were nowhere to be found.

This was probably just as well. The next week a huge limb from a rainforest tree crashed to the ground, smashing the stump and falling across the spot where I would have had my hide. It would not have been healthy to have been there.

Subsequent efforts to find Little Kingfisher nests often began full of promise but invariably ended in disappointment. With practice it is not too difficult to find Little Kingfishers. In north Queensland, it is a bird of lowland rainforest streams with a preference for dark, narrow waterways with plenty of overhanging vegetation.

With John Young, I found numerous birds and also many little circular tunnels dug into rotten trees and into the bases of large epiphytic ferns, holes that could belong only to Little Kingfishers.

In the shadows. Waiting over a rainforest pool, the Little Kingfisher becomes a silhouette.

A dark rainforest creek in northern Queensland, typical breeding habitat of the Little Kingfisher.

Three times John found pairs of birds excavating their holes in similar sites but none were successful: all the nests were abandoned, probably before laying occurred.

Away from the nest I had rather more success. Along the narrow creek where I first saw the bird was a tiny lagoon, closed in by the forest, overhung with vines and littered with fallen branches, all good hunting perches for a kingfisher. Both Little and Azure Kingfishers came here to fish and it seemed a good place to put a hide. We built it on stilts, covering it with palm fronds and siting it in the middle of the lagoon to bring us as close as possible to the likely perches of the tiny kingfisher. It worked and, on several days, we had birds hunting within 10 metres of the hide. Even this

Hinchinbrook Channel in north Queensland. Little Kingfishers of all ages are common here in winter.

distance was rather too far for satisfactory photography but it gave excellent views of their highly idiosyncratic fishing technique. Like the Azure, the Little Kingfisher bobs as it watches for prey but, unlike the Azure, it bobs with its wings as well as with its head, half opening them as it goes up and closing them as it goes down again. Possibly this serves to startle fish and make them move, a similar tactic to the stirring foot movements of some egrets.

It is July 1993 at Hinchinbrook Channel. This maze of tortuous channels running through mangroves is my other place to find Little Kingfishers. It is the middle of the dry and five months away from the birds' reputed breeding season. Nevertheless, the birds are here in some numbers.

It is high water when we arrive but the tide is just beginning to ebb. No kingfishers of any sort are to be seen but having been in mangroves before I know what to expect. With the sea flooding the whole forest, the birds can go anywhere but, as the water falls, they are forced back to the deep channels. We have to wait. As the water drops, the mud banks begin to emerge, revealing the maze of gutters draining back towards the main channel. Crabs and mudskippers start to appear and from all around comes the plop of mangrove seeds dropping from the trees and spearing into the mud.

The boat rounds a bend and there is the first Little Kingfisher, perched among the tangled roots, just above the water. We cut the engine and drift slowly towards it but photography is not easy from a moving platform and the bird is away while I am still struggling for focus.

A little farther along the channel, we find another kingfisher and then another and another. Many of them show the faint barring on the crown characteristic of the juvenile. They are along every waterway, particularly the narrow ones, spaced out every few hundred metres and always alone, as though holding their own stretch of hunting territory. Unfortunately, this abundance does not flow through to the photography and the movement of the boat continues to be a barrier to taking good pictures.

I have always wanted to return to Hinchinbrook in the breeding season to see if the population stays constant. I suspect, however, that as with the Azure Kingfisher, the Little Kingfisher's presence in the mangroves is a transient phenomenon with a movement of birds from fresh to salt water only as fish numbers drop in the freshwater streams and some of the creeks dry up altogether. No doubt some Little Kingfishers do stay to breed but it would be a nightmare place to work, accessible only by boat and with entry to the forest barred by tide and mangrove roots. If that is not enough, the mangroves are home to myriad mosquitoes and a healthy population of saltwater crocodiles. With no wish to become food for either, I must find my nesting Little Kingfishers elsewhere.

In 1998 I twice came close. Pairs at Daintree and Ingham both brought out young but they nested in January at the height of a very wet wet season, which made the creeks they were nesting on inaccessible at the critical time.

Little Kingfisher in the mangroves, a favourite habitat. The scalloped appearance of the blue on the crown shows it is a young bird.

CHAPTER THREE
LAUGHING KOOKABURRA

Dusk thickens at the edge of the forest. It is half an hour after sunset and most of the birds are now silent. But not all! "Koo koo koo koo yok yok yok yok kow kow kow kow". The call rings out through the forest. At once another one of the group takes up the call, then another and a fourth and a fifth, all shouting and yokking and kooking together in a dis- cordant cacophony of sound. For a few moments there is silence and then, from across the valley, come the neighbours' raucous replies in what is very clearly an avian shouting match. It is a common sound in the bush, likely to happen at any time of the day but never more vigorously than in that final chorus before the silence of the night.

The kangaroo! The koala! The kookaburra! Together, these three make up what is probably the best known and loved trio of all Australian animals. The kookaburra! Clown of the bush! The exuberant humorist who sees the funny side of everything, particularly prone to bursting into screams of maniacal laughter at the sight of some human mishap. This is a common perception but is also, of course, a total nonsense, an anthropomorphic creation of the human mind, which loves to see itself mirrored in other creatures: in penguins, in owls, in pigs, sheep, bears and monkeys. In kookaburras.

Not everybody sees kookaburras in such a favourable light. A good friend of mine calls them Laughing Murderers. She has watched them slaughtering the wrens and finches that come to her bird table and doesn't like it but her label is as fallacious and anthropomorphic as is the picture of the clown.

Both pictures may be wrong but anything that raises our awareness of the natural world must surely be good. The Laughing Kookaburra is a celebrity and if the reasons for this are specious, it hardly seems to matter.

If kookaburras are celebrities with people, they are certainly seen as villains by the rest of the bird world. In the forests where I live, only owls and goshawks stimulate more noise and panic among the small birds. Miners and other honeyeaters respond to a kookaburra's every move with a chorus of alarm calls and, as with owls, the progression of noise through the forest is an accurate indicator of the kookaburra's whereabouts.

24

Ever-watchful for the slightest sign of prey, a hunting Laughing Kookaburra waits. There is a lot of waiting in a kingfishers' life.

The Laughing Kookaburra is not only Australia's largest kingfisher but vies with the Giant Kingfisher of Africa for the title of biggest kingfisher in the world. With most groups of birds and animals, the largest species are less common than the small ones but, strangely, this does not apply to the Laughing Kookaburra which, in many parts of Australia, is not only common but easily out-numbers all other kingfisher species added together.

In my home district of south-eastern Victoria, I estimate that there is a family of kookaburras to about every 10 hectares of suitable forest and woodland. In summer it shares this habitat with another dry-land kingfisher, the Sacred, but the Sacred never achieves the same numbers as the kookaburra, seeming to need about five times the area to support a pair. In winter the kookaburras are on their own, for the Sacred Kingfishers are summer visitors, staying only long enough to raise their young before migrating north again.

Why is this? Both species appear to catch much the same sort of food: skinks, spiders, worms and a variety of insects. Certainly the kookaburra does catch mice and birds but the birds are mostly nestlings and are available only for a relatively short season. Snakes are also on the menu but the Laughing Kookaburra takes many fewer than the Blue-winged Kookaburra. I am not sure of the answer but I do get the impression that the Laughing Kookaburra is a much more versatile feeder than the Sacred Kingfisher. Whereas Sacreds catch many skinks for their young, the items of food that kookaburras bring to the nest tend to be tiny, their lack of bulk counterbalanced by the very frequent visits of parents and their helpers.

One characteristic of the Laughing Kookaburra that has helped it to achieve such familiarity is its ready acceptance of people. Much of my kookaburra photography was done at the Cape Conran camping park in eastern Victoria but this is typical of a host of sites in other places.

It was never difficult to find the birds there. My usual routine was to choose a picnic table, set up camera, tripod and flashes and unwrap the butcher's minced meat. By that time, the first kookaburras had usually arrived, sometimes only one but, more usually, two, three or four. It was a wonderful opportunity to see the birds at really close quarters. Usually I went in winter and, with hunger as the driving force, the birds would go anywhere, flying through light beams and flashes to land in the place of my choice. Wildlife photographers are rarely so privileged.

Four Laughing Kookaburras. Family bonds are extremely strong.

Kookaburras, along with all kingfishers, have superb vision, which is the key to their remarkable hunting skills. The technique is to sit on an elevated perch and then watch and wait. Sometimes the perch is only as elevated as a farm fence and the prey is a spider directly beneath it. While there is nothing particularly special about this, sometimes the perch is 10 metres high, the sun has already set and the prey is 200 metres away. This is a favourite hunting time.

Launching from the perch, the kookaburra settles at once into a long, slow glide, arrow-straight, wings quite still, gradually approaching the ground. Only at the last moment is there a furious back-pedalling of wings and the kookaburra lands softly, seizing the prey with its beak at the same instant that its feet touch the ground. I have watched this often and marvelled. Usually the prey is no bigger than a grasshopper or a cricket, tiny creatures that I could never spot at that distance, even with the aid of powerful binoculars.

Once anything is captured in that huge bill, there is no escape. I once suffered a kookaburra seizing hold of my finger and can attest to the beak's crushing power. Unlike raptors, which catch prey with their talons and use the beak only for killing, kookaburras use their beaks for the whole process. Theirs is not a tearing or biting bill, it is a gripping one; but the technique is brutally effective. Trapped in the bill's vice, the prey is carried to a nearby tree and beaten lifeless against a branch. If the victim is a snake or a lizard, it is usually the head that is hit. With invertebrates, it does not seem to matter, and they are frequently legless by the time the kookaburra stops.

Just occasionally, a kookaburra's recognition of potential prey fails and I have seen one pounce on a stray swimming pool thermometer and proceed to pound it against a concrete slab. Fortunately, the kookaburra realised its error before too much damage had been done, either to the thermometer or to the bird's digestive system.

Kookaburras are usually regarded as dry-land kingfishers and this is almost universally correct. However, along the Murray River, my friend Lindsay Cupper came across a group of Laughing Kookaburras that habitually dived into the water in pursuit of fish and now I have reports of others in East Gippsland that do the same. It is a performance I have yet to witness but it is looking ever more likely that most Australian kingfishers are able to dive into water for food if the opportunity presents itself. Many of them would rarely have this opportunity but, anatomically, most of them look capable of it. I have watched both Sacred and Forest Kingfishers dive successfully for fish and, hunting through the tidal mangroves, the Collared must surely do the same. Only the Buff-breasted Paradise-Kingfisher, with its flowing tail plumes, seems an unlikely candidate to be plunging into water.

My own property is just 100 hectares in extent. Most of this is open pasture but it is surrounded by forest and a perimeter walk takes me through the territories of no fewer than six families of kookaburras. Throughout the 15 years I have known them the territories have not changed, but this stable state has been achieved only through constant bellicose declarations of ownership by every group there.

This goes on throughout the year but it is in August, with breeding approaching, that it is at its most obvious. Then they augment their vocal outbursts with conspicuous boundary patrol flights, paired birds following each other in line ahead, stiff-winged with slow deep beats, marking the limits of their territory. It is a defensive display, not invasive, but without it, invasion of their own territory would probably soon follow.

The family I know best has two nest holes 300 metres apart, both of which have been used successfully a number of times. Nevertheless, it seems that birds are constantly on the lookout for new holes with nest-site potential. One such spot is in a mahogany tree right outside my bedroom window. On a winter's morning in 1994, I heard the low, chuckling conversational call of a kookaburra. It was just after dawn and, in the half light, two kookaburras were perched on a dead stick close to the mahogany. One bird glided down to the trunk of the tree, perched there and pecked a few times. Then

Three Laughing Kookaburra chicks, all about three weeks old.

it went back to the dead stick and the other bird flew down to the same spot and did the same thing. They stayed there for two or three minutes, taking turns to peck at the tree, always in exactly the same spot. When they left, I walked over to the tree. Three metres up was the elliptical scar where a limb had fallen away. One day, it would become the entrance to a hollow but that looked to be a long way off.

The next morning the kookaburras were back, and again the next, always arriving before sunrise, making three or four sorties to the tree and then leaving. It was clear that they were very interested in the site but equally clear that they had no hope of excavating a hole there. I set out to help them.

It was not hard work. The base of the old fallen limb had already rotted back into the trunk of the tree and, like a dentist working on a carious tooth, I was able to clean out the cavity with hammer and chisel. I hoped that it was big enough because the living wood beyond the cavity was ebony-hard and extremely difficult to remove inside the hollow.

The next day the birds arrived as usual and there was much chuckling when they discovered that they had a cavity. In turn, they perched at the entrance and looked inside but did not enter. Through late July and August they never missed a day and I felt sure they would use it. On 20 August, four birds attended the hole together and, a week later, the two senior birds were mating at the top of a nearby electricity pole. That was their undoing. Early in September I realised they were no longer coming to the hole and then I found one of the birds dead below the power pole. One bird could perch there with impunity but a copulating pair was likely to bridge the gap across the high-voltage wires. For the rest of 1994, the hole was abandoned.

Perhaps the bird that died had been the moving force. The kookaburras formed a new pair and, in 1995, rarely visited the site. In 1996 and 1997, they came a little more but went away and nested in another hole a few hundred metres away. As the 1998 season approaches, they are looking again. The hole is now big enough for them to go inside, turn round and come out again. Whether or not that is sufficient remains to be seen.

In 1996 I photographed their neighbours nesting. Their hole was also in a mahogany and there were five adults looking after the three young. As each adult approached, it called with a rattling chuckle and then perched before making the final gliding approach. Sometimes two, or even three would arrive more or less simultaneously, setting off much murmuring and chuckling among

Top left: The Laughing Kookaburra comes in to land with tail down and feet thrown forward.
Top right: With its feet almost on the ground, the bird reduces speed with stalled wings.
Left: Touchdown.

This Laughing Kookaburra is one of a pair which nest regularly in an upturned canoe hanging in a barn.
The prey is a small snake.

The watchful eye. Despite their proximity to people, the kookaburras remain very wary around their nest.

themselves as they decided which of them would come in first. The chicks were already 10 days old when I found the nest, big enough to snatch the food the moment it appeared at the entrance and the adults stayed there just long enough for that to happen, only once going briefly inside, to brood the young.

Kookaburras make almost no effort to disguise where they are breeding and are noisier around the nest than almost any other bush bird. Sometimes, after feeding, two adults would land close by and shout their calls to the skies with upstretched heads and quivering bills, cackling and shrieking as though they wanted to tell the whole world that this was where they had their nest.

In its final approach to seize prey, the Laughing Kookaburra's wingspread would do justice to an eagle.

The life of kookaburras makes a fascinating study but each new observation tends to pose as many new questions as it answers. With shouting matches, for example, some of their purposes are clear but why have they taken on such a complex and predictable pattern? When it comes to territory defence, it seems logical that two birds must give out a stronger signal than one and that this will continue to be reinforced by every new voice. But why is the pattern so constant?

I have watched it so many times. A kookaburra flies alone through the trees, glides up to a bare branch and stops. It has not gone unobserved and a second bird appears from another direction, gliding in to land beside the first to be greeted with a muted chuckle. That is the signal and more kookaburras converge on the spot to break at once into the characteristic shrieking and cackling.

Is this all for the benefit of the neighbours? Possibly it is but I feel that it is more than this: a ritual meeting that strengthens the bond within the group and helps to familiarise the younger members with the characteristics of the territory.

Then there are the helpers at the nest. Why does it take one, two or three extra adults to enable the biological parents to raise the young? Unknown in most parts of the world, it is a very Australian characteristic and occurs too with White-winged Choughs, Apostle Birds, blue wrens and babblers. In fact, around 80 Australian bird species are recorded as having helpers at the nest or some form of cooperative feeding. Many reasons have been put forward and probably all are correct. The helpers are, of course, younger birds than the parents and, with small and tightly held territories, there are few new sites for them to set up on their own. By taking on the role of helper, they are finding them-selves some space to live, gaining experience for when they breed themselves and assisting the parents in a task that two birds might find impossible on their own.

This last point has come to light through the work of Rob Heinsohn on White-winged Choughs. He found that it was only with the aid of helpers that the choughs were able to raise a full brood and that, unassisted, the parents either failed or could raise only one young. The reason

An adult Laughing Kookaburra bringing food to the nest. This pair raised their single chick on their own with no helpers.

With young to feed, a Laughing Kookaburra swoops up to its nest in a Southern Mahogany.

seemed to be the difficulty in finding enough food in the dry Australian forest, a task beyond the abilities of an unassisted pair.

Extrapolated to kookaburras, this gives an explanation for the existence of helpers and a clue to some other kookaburra puzzles, such as the small territories and dense populations compared with Sacred Kingfishers. With several adults all feeding the young, there is no need to range so far in search of food. Also, those adults are having to find food for only one brood, not for two or three as would a similar number of Sacred Kingfishers. Against this, however, is the point that Sacred Kingfishers are often double brooded, something I have not yet encountered with kookaburras.

It was always thought that the helpers at kookaburra nests were the young of the adult pair, gaining experience against the time when they would replace their parents. However, David Curl, in his innovative work on Blue-winged Kookaburras, has found that this is not always so. Almost routinely, the biological young of the adult pair are augmented by young from a neighbouring group, kidnapped as fledglings and enticed to remain with their adoptive family. It is a system that clearly has genetic benefits and, of course, also happens in reverse with young from the kidnapping family being lost to other groups.

Leaving the nest tree. This dark-headed bird is one of the helpers and not a parent of the young.

The Vantage Point. Many
Laughing Kookaburras have
grown accustomed to people
and will perch almost anywhere
in their search for food.

Whether or not this happens in Laughing Kookaburras is not yet known but, with so much of
the two species' behaviour being similar, it seems highly likely. Kidnapping has always been thought
to be rare in nature but it is a difficult thing to spot and will only be recognised through very careful
observation. Perhaps it is not rare at all. Heinsohn noted it with his White-winged Choughs and it
may be a practice that is far more widespread than previously suspected.

One aspect of kingfisher life that I wanted to record was the activities inside a nest, and the con-
fiding kookaburra seemed likely to be a good subject. I chose the 1996 nest and, after the young had
flown, cut a square block out of the back of the nest hollow where I could eventually put camera and
flash. With the block replaced and the cracks sealed, I then had to wait for the next nesting season.
The birds had not been disturbed, the hole looked unchanged and I had high hopes they would use it.
    They didn't. In early September 1997, I realised they were using an alternative and much higher
site a short distance away. However, it was not my activities that had made them change. Looking
closely at the abandoned hollow, I noticed a sprig of dry bracken. There was more than a sprig and,
climbing to the nest, I found the complete hollow packed with bracken. A Ring-tailed Possum had
made this home and, even though it had now gone, the kookaburras were not going to use a hollow
in that condition. I removed the bracken to wait in hope for the next season.

CHAPTER FOUR
BLUE-WINGED KOOKABURRA

The Blue-winged Kookaburra is a bird of many conspicuous features but the most striking of all must surely be its voice. Graham Pizzey, in his *Field Guide to the Birds of Australia*, describes it as "appalling". Some people may find this a little severe but there is no denying the overwhelming power and penetration of the Blue-winged Kookaburra's call, a series of explosive "Yoks", which give place to a string of discordant howls, shrieks and cackles, all delivered at ear-splitting volume. It may not be everybody's favourite bird song but it is one of the sounds of northern Australia, familiar to almost everyone who has spent time in that part of the country.

Rarely does a Blue-winged Kookaburra call alone. Their lives are centred on the family, which stays together and defends a territory throughout the year. The bigger the family, the stronger is the hold on the territory and one very good way to maintain that hold is to declare it vocally. Thus, the call of the lone Blue-wing moves on rapidly to the shrieking, shouting cacophony of the whole family in full voice. There is also a visual side to these choruses and it is a common sight to see several birds sitting close together on some prominent perch, heads thrown back, tails cocked, beaks pointed skywards and throats pulsing as they scream out defiance to their neighbours.

If there is another Blue-winged Kookaburra territory nearby, then the owners are bound to reply. I have known two or three other territories to be within earshot and the forest to ring with the maniacal voices of the rival owners, all claiming their proprietorship together. As with the Laughing Kookaburra, these performances are most prone to take place at dawn and dusk but they are not confined to these times and, during the breeding season, neighbourhood shouting matches may continue right through the day.

Visually, the Blue-winged is not hard to distinguish from the Laughing Kookaburra. The two species share the same long-billed, short-tailed silhouette but, even at a distance, the bill looks bigger, the neck longer and the body leaner, exaggerating the top-heavy appearance. It is a paler yet more colourful bird than the Laughing Kookaburra. The head is white, streaked with black as though with a fine comb, and the neck and underparts are close to pure white. There is much more blue in the wings than the Laughing and, unlike that species, all sexes and ages have a blue rump. One other singular feature of the Blue-winged Kookaburra is the white eye, peculiar to this species

Blue-winged Kookaburra at the nest. The white eye makes the gaze seem very cold and penetrating.

In flight from the nest tree. The blue tail shows this Blue-winged Kookaburra to be a male.

among all the world's kingfishers. This gives a cold and fish-like aura but may well enhance the bird's visual acuity for, in a group of birds renowned for their keen vision, the Blue-wing's seems to be particularly sharp.

In size, power, diet, nest preference and general aggressiveness, the two species of kookaburra seem remarkably similar. In southern Australia, there are only Laughing Kookaburras and, across the north, only Blue-wings but, through much of Queensland, the two species occur together. It is unusual for two species to occupy exactly the same ecological niche and I have been puzzled to know what it is that separates them. Against the many similarities, it does seem that the Blue-wing prefers the drier, more open woodlands and that, where the two occur together, the Laughing is more likely to be in denser forest, unlike its position farther south, where it too is a bird of woodland. Possibly, where both species occur, the Blue-wing is dominant; it is certainly the more common bird through much of north Queensland.

Even if the Blue-winged is dominant among kookaburras, it is certainly the shyer of the two species when it comes to contact with humans. In the bush, it is very difficult to approach and, even when perched on powerlines beside country roads, it seems it rarely becomes used to traffic, usually flying back to the protection of the bush long before an approaching vehicle comes anywhere near. At the nest it is a similar story and the Blue-winged Kookaburra is the only species of kingfisher that has caused me problems as a result of its shyness.

Like many kingfishers of northern Australia, the Blue-winged Kookaburra frequently chooses to nest in a termite mound, never on the ground but always in a tree. However, this is only one option and many pairs breed in tree hollows, with a particular liking for the smooth-mouthed holes in Poplar Gums.

A termite mound that will accommodate a kookaburra family needs to be a large one and only the biggest are suitable. However, not every kookaburra seems able to gauge the necessary size and many excavations are begun only for the birds to come up against solid timber or to drill right through the mound. These abortive assaults cause little harm either to kookaburras or termites. The thin crust and honeycomb interior of the mound are easily breached by the kookaburra's bill and it does not take the termites long to repair the abandoned hole.

Nevertheless, it does take a certain amount of effort for a kookaburra to dig a nest in a termite mound. The beauty of the tree-hollow site is that it is ready made. I have had hides at five different Blue-winged Kookaburra nests, all in tree hollows. At one of these, the birds were extraordinarily shy and, despite their accepting the unoccupied hide for a full two weeks, would never come to the nest once I was inside. A second pair was also perpetually wary, while at a third nest there was little activity because the young had not yet hatched. Fortunately, the remaining two pairs more than compensated for the problems I had with the others.

The first of these was in an unlikely site: a hollow in a mango tree less than 2 metres above the ground and inside a set of stockyards that was frequently occupied by cattle. The cattle seemed not to worry the kookaburras, which have nested there annually at least since 1991 and possibly for some years before that.

I first saw this nest in November 1992. There had been two eggs but only one had hatched and the young kookaburra, about 17 days old, sat there with the addled egg beside it. In shape the chick

A Blue-winged Kookaburra rests, panting, after flying to the nest. The brown tail marks this kookaburra as either a female or a young male.

was all kingfisher, but it gave a decidedly reptilian impression too. Like all baby kingfishers, it had no down and the dark grey quills of the sheathed feathers grew straight out of the pink, naked skin. Within just a few days, the fully coloured feathers would burst from these sheaths and the strange, primeval-looking creature would undergo an almost instant transformation to the shimmering beauty of a near full-sized kookaburra.

Three adults were caring for the chick: a fully coloured male, a female and a young male helper, easily distinguished by having only the outer feathers blue in an otherwise brown tail. Both species of kookaburra use helpers at the nest. These are immature birds of both sexes which, in time, may inherit the territory. At this nest in both 1992 and 1996, there was only one helper but I have known Laughing Kookaburra pairs to be assisted by at least three helpers and possibly more. I took a lot of flight photographs at this nest but, what with cattle, mud and stockyard fences, it was hardly the most photogenic of sites and I turned my attentions elsewhere.

The second site was a billabong, a classic of its kind. It was a bow-shaped waterhole, a kilometre in length and cut off from the main river, except at times of flood. Around its banks grew tall paperbarks interspersed with pandanus, and one huge, spreading fig. Jacanas ran across the waterlilies but the billabong was drying rapidly and there would be little water left at the end of the dry season. At this time, however, it was a different story and the richness and the profusion of birdlife was quite astonishing.

In 1996, the billabong appeared to hold two pairs of Blue-winged Kookaburras, one at each end. We approached from the north and were met by a cackling and very territorial trio. There had been a nest here last year and it seemed they must be breeding again but a search of every available hollow revealed nothing.

Arriving at the nest, with wings back and feet thrust forward.

A Blue-winged Kookaburra in full flight from the nest tree.

Left: With a grasshopper in its bill, the Blue-winged Kookaburra crouches before springing vertically to the nest. Below: On a hunting foray, this adult has caught a frog for its young, picking up some foliage in the process.

Magpie Geese in their thousands watched us nervously from the waterlilies, necks upstretched, muscles tensed, judging the moment when they should flee. Then the first birds broke ranks and, in a great roar of wings, they were away, a packed, honking phalanx of black and white. They would not go far for there was little fresh water left in the district.

Then Bush Stone-curlews began to appear out of the shadows: stealthy, creeping. For such large birds they can be remarkably cryptic. They emerged from behind logs and the shade of trees, bird after bird until I was able to count more than 60. Then they, too, began to leave, their flight as furtive as their walking, a brief run followed by a silent launch, low to the ground, necks and legs outstretched, wings stiff and angled with only the white patches in the tips breaking the dull ground colour of their plumage. At night, Bush Stone-curlews can be among the noisiest of birds but these, disturbed by day, uttered not a sound.

The other party of Blue-winged Kookaburras was nesting at the southern end of the billabong. Nearby, the fig tree was heavily in fruit and full of birds: pigeons, Koels, orioles, drongos, figbirds and at least 20 of those huge, strange birds, the Channel-billed Cuckoos. They flew in like great seabirds, greeting each other with loud raucous braying and then disappearing into the leafy obscurity of the fig tree's canopy. The fig was close to the kookaburras' nest tree and my time in the hide would be spent to the frequent accompaniment of Channel-bills' trumpetings.

All the way down the billabong we had checked every hollow for signs of kookaburras. Barking Owls had nested here last year but we found only bones and feathers in one hole and if they had bred at all their season was already over. Suddenly three kookaburras were all shrieking and cackling at once and, six metres up in a paperbark, we found a hollow with one nestling and an addled egg. The chick's eyes were just open and it looked to be about a week old.

We walked away and waited. Within minutes, the male appeared, carrying a slender snake in his bill. The female saw him coming and flew to the hole first, waiting for him and seizing the snake as he landed. She took it inside and I could not see just how the baby was fed. The next day, we brought in the tower and, on the third day, I was ready to start watching from the hide.

All earlier Blue-winged Kookaburras I had worked with had been extremely wary but these birds were a most welcome exception as my field notes from the time attest:

November 7, 1996
9.15 a.m. John Young has only just left and, already, there are harsh, low squawks nearby and I can hear the chattering of Willy Wagtails as they harass their old enemy. In front of me is a bow-shaped branch, its bark rubbed smooth from many landings. Just below the level of the nest, this is the final take-off point for the approaching kookaburras.
9.20 a.m. Now the female is on the perch, eyeing the hide intently. There is something very strange about the Blue-winged Kookaburra, beyond its dramatic shape and the iridescent beauty of its plumage. It is the cold, intense stare of the small white eye, which gives the impression it can see through anything, even the thickest of fabrics. Fortunately, it seems she cannot penetrate this canvas and, after studying the hide for some minutes, she flies to the hole and feeds her baby. Now there is no hesitation from any of the adults and, in the next two and a half hours, there are 16 visits. I think there are three birds, one male and two females but, in the brief time that they are at the nest, it is hard to be sure. Each visit to the nest is heralded by a soft, wheezing call, "Wow".

I spent four days in the hide at this nest and the adults packed their solitary chick with an astonishing amount of food. On 8 November, they came in 23 times in just over four hours. Much of the

Two baby Blue-winged Kookaburras, only a day or two old, quite naked and with eyes not yet open.

prey was small: worms, spiders, phasmids and insect pupae. There were, however, plenty of bigger items too, including frogs, yabbies and, over the four days, a total of nine snakes, some of which were more than 30 centimetres long. Clearly the prey was taken in a variety of situations, for the phasmids would have to be plucked from the foliage while the kookaburras' occasional blackened breasts bore witness to the muddy medium where they caught the yabbies.

Even when the kookaburras were quiet, there was always something happening at this most fascinating of billabongs. A dingo trotted along the water's edge, scattering the geese in honking indignation. The arrival of a White-bellied Sea-Eagle caused a more serious panic and the air was filled with birds: ducks, spoonbills, herons and waders as well as the geese. Fortunately for them, the sea-eagle's eye was on more static prey and it sailed down to snatch a hapless tortoise from the log where it had been sunning itself.

For me, a less welcome diversion was the arrival of a cow, who insinuated herself under one of my guy ropes and proceeded to rub her back up and down against the rope while the whole tower swayed and bucked until I thought it must come down. Miraculously it stood but, when the cow left, the rope was hanging slack, making the tower so unstable that it toppled and went to fall as I climbed down. Fortunately, there was enough purchase left in the rope to prevent it from coming down completely and it stopped at a drunken angle, leaving me to complete a somewhat precarious descent to the ground. It was my last session with the birds and, with the tower already half down, we had only to complete the lowering and take our equipment away.

It would be another three weeks before the young kookaburra left the nest but all the indications were that it had an excellent chance of achieving this. Probably the kookaburras would have used the same hole in 1997, but this was a desirable piece of avian real estate and they were not the only prospective tenants. There is a pecking order among hole nesters and, when a pair of Barking Owls took over the hollow, there was nothing the kookaburras could do about it. At least the owls made good use of their new home and, like the kookaburras before them, were successful in raising their brood.

Above: At nearly four weeks of age, the young Blue-winged Kookaburra has a distinctly reptilian appearance. Right: The cow that wrapped itself round a guy rope and nearly brought down my tower.

CHAPTER FIVE
FOREST KINGFISHER

It was the noise that drew my attention: a harsh, rattling trill, followed by the sound of a single impact, like the strike of a hammer against wood. Then silence. After half a minute, the sequence was repeated and then again. It came from nearly 300 metres away but through the open tropical woodland it was not hard to trace the source.

Perched on a dead limb of a eucalypt was a bright blue kingfisher. I spotted it just as it took off to fly fast and flat, straight at the pitted surface of an arboreal termite mound only 10 metres away. In full flight, it hit the mound with its beak, sending chips of the outer casing tumbling to the ground. I thought back to the Yellow-billed Kingfisher doing the same thing and it seemed inconceivable that a bird could do this and suffer no harm. However, there it was, already in full flight back to the perch. Certainly, there have been instances of kingfishers breaking their necks while doing this and, knowing how easily they can kill themselves by flying into windows, it is surprising that it does not happen more often.

This was a Forest Kingfisher and I could see now that it was a female. For a few seconds she rested on the dead stick and then she was on her way again, wings thrashing to work up maximum speed before the jarring impact against the mound. This time, she clung to it afterwards, digging with her bill at the crater in its surface. Then she let go, falling and spinning all in one movement to return to the perch and begin the next cycle. Each flight was signalled by the trill and then, just as she hit the mound, she gave a short sharp call of "Tac", very similar to the call given by the Sacred Kingfisher when prospecting a new nest site.

For half an hour she continued to batter the mound, making more than 30 flights. By the time she stopped there was a deep cavity on the surface and termites were emerging from the hole, but it would still need another day's digging before she was into the mound's honeycombed interior.

Many Australian kingfishers make their nests in termite mounds, some invariably, some often and others only occasionally. Arboreal mounds are used by both species of kookaburra and by Yellow-billed, Collared, Sacred, Forest and, possibly, Red-backed kingfishers. The Buff-breasted Paradise-Kingfisher nests in terrestrial mounds and it is only the Azure and Little that nest exclusively in other places.

With a frog in his bill, a male Forest Kingfisher comes to his nest in an arboreal termite mound.

For the kookaburras, with their strong bills, it is an easy task to break into a termite mound, but for the other species it is hard work. The terrestrial mounds used by the Buff-breasted Paradise-Kingfishers are particularly unyielding, but it is not just the texture of the mound that makes the work difficult. Frequently, the excavating bird comes up against solid timber before the hole is deep enough or, at the other extreme, burrows right through the mound and out the other side. In both instances, there is no alternative but to start again and many birds dig a number of holes before they finally get it right. The only two species I have watched digging are the Forest and Yellow-billed Kingfishers, and while the male does some work, most is done by the female. Probably the same applies to the other species but I have no evidence.

Opposite: The gleaming beauty of the male Forest Kingfisher. This bird is unusual in that the white collar is incomplete at the back of the neck. Below: Late afternoon in a Forest Kingfisher's breeding territory in tropical woodland.

Above: Termites are vitally important to many Australian kingfishers. The roof of this termite trail has been lifted to reveal the termites beneath it. Right: The characteristic trail leading to the termite mound. Many Australian kingfishers use these mounds for nesting. Opposite: A male Forest Kingfisher delivers a skink to the nest.

What causes some species of kingfisher to nest in termite mounds while others choose tree hollows? It is a question for which I have no answer but it raises some intriguing points. In southern Australia, the Sacred Kingfishers and Laughing Kookaburras do not have to make the choice as there are very few arboreal termite mounds. For the kookaburras of the tropics, where both types of site are available, it seems to be a matter of personal preference. However, both the Forest and Yellow-billed Kingfishers appear to be termite specific and I have yet to see either species using a tree hollow. One reason for this must be the abundance of termite mounds in the tropics. However, there are also plenty of good tree hollows so there must be other explanations.

Compared to the tree hollow, the termite mound does have its drawbacks. A good tree hollow usually stays more or less unchanged for many years, whereas termite mounds may alter in shape, often fall off the tree and, because of the termites' repair work, need to be dug out every season. Why then do the kingfishers choose them? My supposition is that the tree hollow has two main disadvantages. In the highly competitive environment of the tropics, the hollow may already be occupied or may attract a more powerful intending tenant. Worse still, it is particularly vulnerable to predation by snakes and goannas which, without doubt, are able to remember where they have

Close by his northern Queensland nest, a male Forest Kingfisher rests, panting, in the heat of the day.

previously found prey. For the well-armed kookaburras, the risk is not so great but the smaller king-fishers are safer in a freshly opened termite mound that predators are less likely to visit.

I saw my first Forest Kingfishers many years ago, perched along the telephone wires outside Cairns. They congregate there in the winter in large numbers, sharing the wires with White-breasted Woodswallows. A Forest Kingfisher would look good in any setting but there are better places to watch them.

I began to study them seriously in 1992. Superficially, they seemed quite similar to the Sacred and I expected their behaviour to mirror this kingfisher but I still had much to learn. It was late November and, in the dry tropical woodland of north Queensland, there had been little rain for months. The grass crackled underfoot, the air screamed with the song of cicadas and the bush and its inhabitants seemed in a state of torpor as they waited for the rain.

Nevertheless, Forest Kingfishers were about and on the first day we found three nests. All were in arboreal termite mounds with fresh, clean-cut entrance hollows that could not have been done more neatly with a carpenter's brace and bit. We saw birds at all the nests, sometimes the pair, some-times just one but there was no sign of any activity and we concluded that they had not yet laid.

With no shortage of Forest Kingfishers we found nine more nests over the next four days. At two of these, we saw a bird fly to the entrance and look inside but no bird ever went in or out and it seemed that no eggs had yet been laid. We concluded that drought was the problem and that they were all waiting for the first summer storms to galvanise them into activity.

How easy it is to draw the wrong conclusions! On the night of 23 November, there was rain, not very much but perhaps it would be enough to stimulate the kingfishers to start laying. The next morning, we set out in hope but were quite unprepared for the sight of a Forest Kingfisher swoop-ing up to the nest hole with a tiny skink in its beak. It perched on the mound, thrusting the prey inside and, in the dark interior, something took it. We moved to the base of the tree and, from within the nest, came the muffled, wheezing calls of very small babies.

We had been completely fooled, never having considered the possibility that the kingfishers might not sit on their eggs at all. Once the thought had occurred, it seemed so logical. The interior of the termite mound, warmed by the sun, was a natural incubator, releasing the kingfishers from the need to warm the eggs themselves.

Over the next few days more nests showed evidence of young inside and it was clear that this was no isolated occurrence. I have now watched Forest Kingfishers for several seasons and have only twice seen one come out from a nest. Whether the birds incubate at night is another question and I have never yet been at a nest at dusk to see if this happens. Nor do I know what happens farther south in New South Wales where springtime temperatures are cooler but, in north Queensland at least, there is no question that Forest Kingfishers have found a way to avoid the long task of incubation.

Two mornings later I was in the hide. It was nearly 9 a.m., the sun had been up for three hours and the young must already have been fed several times. They would not have long to wait. The rattling trill heralded the approach of an adult and then it was there, perched 40 metres away with a skink in its bill. It paused, but only for a minute. The soft, musical chirrup told both the young and me that it was on its way and it flew, taking only three seconds to cover the 40 metres to the nest. This was the male, a gleaming study in turquoise, white and black. His tiny feet gripped the lip of the hole and he thrust his bill inside, his tail bending as he braced back against it. The skink disappeared and as he withdrew his bill he was away, dropping and twisting all in one movement.

In three hours that morning, the adults came 11 times with prey, mainly skinks but there were also stick insects and grasshoppers. In the afternoon they went one better and I had 12 visits in about the same time. As with many birds, the visits were not regular. There was a two-hour gap in

Female Forest Kingfisher with cricket. Females always have an incomplete white collar.

the afternoon, followed by three visits in 15 minutes. Other days produced similar patterns but not everything was explicable.

On the second day at 5 p.m. the male had no food but was on his usual perch. He chattered and then flew straight at the mound, smacking into it so hard that pieces of earth were sent flying. He returned to his perch and did it again and then again, seeming almost demented in his furious attack on his own nest. Sometimes he struck the entrance and sometimes the mound above it, each time giving a call like a Silvereye just before he struck. I have seen a Collared Kingfisher do this to dislodge ants but on this occasion there seemed to be no reason for this onslaught, which was repeated 18 times in a few minutes.

The next morning produced more strange behaviour when both adults began to fly noisily at another termite mound 50 metres away, striking it with their bills and going through the motions of excavating a new nest. Then they flew to the very top of a dead tree, facing each other with half-open wings, swaying and chattering. This performance was easier to interpret. A rival kingfisher had appeared and this very clear signal said, "Go away, there's no room for you here."

I could not watch this nest to completion but I photographed at another one in 1997, revelling in the sight of this extraordinarily beautiful kingfisher. Tree frogs were on the menu at this nest and I also saw the female take a skink, travelling like an arrow for 50 metres and snatching it from the ground with scarcely a check in her flight. I had learned a lot since watching those birds on the telephone wires in Cairns.

CHAPTER SIX
RED-BACKED KINGFISHER

The Kingfisher! A colourful word for a colourful bird. The name has its origin in medieval England and, for the early British bird books, it was the only kingfisher: a brilliant blue bird that fished a green and watery landscape.

Applied as it is today to the worldwide group, the name is not always apt and is certainly unsuitable for the Red-backed Kingfisher, the desert kingfisher of Australia. Many of Australia's kingfishers have no direct need of water but the endemic Red-backed is the most successfully adapted of them all. Its home is the hot, dry and harsh inland, a hostile terrain which it shares with Grasswrens, crows and desert falcons. Only when breeding has finished will some birds make a concession to a less spartan world and move towards the coast for a few months of the dry season.

Above: Portrait of a male Red-backed Kingfisher. His blues are perceptibly brighter than the female's.
Opposite below: Red-backed Kingfisher perched against the red sand of the desert. This is the female, with a darker crown than the male.

I have seen Red-backs perched incongruously on the telephone wires of coastal north Queensland. I have also seen them far inland, nesting among the roots of upturned trees in the Victorian Mallee and in the dry gullies along the Strzelecki Track.

All of these were incidental sightings when I was not really following kingfishers at all and, to study the Red-back, I went elsewhere, travelling due west from the Queensland coast at Townsville and out to the country around Mount Isa. The two-day journey is an ecological transect of north Queensland, moving from the lush, tropical coastal belt through eucalypt forest, dry woodland, grassland, open plain and finally to the stony landscape of Mount Isa.

Along the way Red-backed Kingfishers were tunnelling into the vertical banks beside the highway where the bulldozers had taken earth for roadworks. Accustomed to traffic, the birds here might have accepted us very quickly but the sites were noisy, visually unattractive and certainly too public to be leaving camera equipment unattended.

On the first night, John Young and I camped by a dry creek on a blacksoil plain south of Hughenden. It was a flat, flood-prone place where the ground existed in only two states: fine bulldust when it was dry or thick black mud when it rained. It took only one heavy shower to produce the latter and we were not going to take the risk of staying there for long. At dusk there were few birds to be seen of any sort but the next morning we were surprised by the alto piping of a Red-backed Kingfisher, an unmistakable call that carries above the sound of the wind and other background noises.

We saw him at once, perched conspicuously on a dead twig, calling up to 10 times a minute, each call a single, level oboe note. The call proclaimed his territory and he launched himself, wings flailing to gain speed and then raking back in the final approach as he sent a guiltless wood-swallow fleeing from its perch. He returned to another vantage point and then set off again, a winged arrow, this time with a much larger Magpie Lark as his target. Each time he flew, he signalled his intentions with a grating chatter but this call was not purely aggressive and seemed to prefix most forms of activity by both sexes.

At this point the female gave the same call and dived across the creek towards us, disappearing into dead ground behind the near bank. I thought she was hunting but she did not reappear and, after she had eventually flown up, we walked round to find a freshly dug hole. It was a third of the way up the two-metre vertical bank, going in where the ground was hard and stony, unlike the Azure Kingfisher, which always seems to prefer to tunnel just below the top of the bank. The hole went in for more than 40 centimetres, sloping gently upwards to a large chamber. On the ground below the entrance was a pile of fine, fresh soil, kicked out by the kingfishers during their digging. There were no eggs but laying could not have been far away and, 10 minutes after we left, both birds were back at work at the tunnel. It was 22 September.

This was not our final destination. We knew that Red-backed Kingfishers were much more plentiful farther inland, and here there was the added risk of being trapped by rain. We continued westward.

For the first-time visitor, the landscape near Mount Isa comes as a surprise. It is a rough, dry, broken terrain of incredible beauty. Out of the plains rise a series of weathered sandstone hills, their slopes carpeted with the rounded tussocks of spinifex and strewn with flat boulders split from the layered sandstone. Clinging to the slopes are the slender Ghost Gums, graceful little trees with white trunks and bright green foliage, a dramatic contrast to the red of the sandstone.

We knew where we were heading and followed a narrow track, winding in among the hills. This is remote country and the only sign of human presence was the track and a long-abandoned copper mine, its equipment gradually rusting back into the landscape. At the end of the track a dam, put in to supply the mine, held the only water for kilometres around. We camped there for the next 10 days without seeing another human being.

It takes time to become familiar with a new district but John had been here two weeks before and had found Red-backs going into a tunnel in the bank of a dry sandstone gully just below the dam. At that time the birds had been calling frequently but on our first afternoon there was neither sight nor sound of them. At the nest there were strands of spider's web across the hole, a little whitewash on the ground and a broken eggshell in the entrance. This nest had either been predated or the young had already flown.

We returned early the next morning. A pair of Crested Pigeons flew in on singing wings, making for a soak below the dam, and a Spinifex Pigeon came the same way on foot, its lovely russet plumage

Two Red-backed Kingfishers rest after digging their nest hole. The lower bird is the male.

In the mine shaft. Four aspects of the Red-backed Kingfishers' flight to and from the nest hole.

Red boulders, Ghost Gums and spinifex. The beauty of Red-backed Kingfisher territory south of Mount Isa.

blending in with the red of the sand. It was 7 a.m. before the male Red-back showed himself, piping from a dead tree before flying to the female, who had been perched silently and unobtrusively nearby. For a minute they perched together and then flew, the male leading his mate down into the dry gully. I could not see into the gully but they were there for an hour before the male flew up again. When I walked in, the female emerged from a new hole a short distance from the first one. It already went in for more than 40 centimetres although the chamber had not yet been excavated.

This nest proved something of an enigma. I never saw a bird come out again and no eggs were laid but the male continued to call and chase away intruders and the spiders never put a web across the entrance. Some other species of kingfisher partially or completely dig their nest holes and then rest before continuing and it seems likely that this was happening here.

Fortunately, this was not the only pair of Red-backs in the district. Nowhere else have I ever found so many, and standing on top of some of the hills it was sometimes possible to hear the calls of three different males – on a still day these calls will carry for a full kilometre. They are territorial calls and were likely to lead us to the nest site. We set out across the hills towards one of them.

We had not gone far before we realised the calls were leading us towards an old mine shaft. They stopped before we arrived there and we surveyed the old workings. Around the shaft lay a few remnants of mining history: rusty winding gear, a shattered concrete slab, baulks of timber, sheets of iron. There was no sign of a road and it must all have been brought in by packhorse. The top of the shaft was quite square, its hand-hewn sides mathematically perpendicular. I dropped a stone and listened. From the delay before it reached the bottom, the shaft must have been at least 30 metres deep.

We did not have to look far for the kingfishers' nest hole and there was not one but seven. They were all on one side of the shaft, mostly about two metres from the top and of varying ages, some of them disused and crumbling but at least two looking fresh enough to be this season's. I had no desire

In their breeding territories, male Red-backed Kingfishers call from prominent perches.

to end my days at the bottom of a mine shaft and, having no climbing gear, we made a mental note of the site and went looking for more accessible holes.

It was not too difficult. The mine shaft had been the clue and now it became a question of searching for old mines rather than looking for the kingfishers directly. It worked. We found four more occupied mine shafts plus another two nests in roadside cuttings, all of them man-made sites. Only our very first nest in the dry gully was in a natural setting.

Some of the old mines were quite hard to find, high on the hillsides and hidden by folds in the ground. The piping calls of the kingfishers often gave the first clue, carrying with great clarity when the air was still. It seemed strange to find the birds in such places but, with the absence of suitable natural nesting sites, I had no doubt that the mining had helped at least this species.

Not all the mines had deep shafts and at one that had fallen in I was able to climb down and inspect the nests. I hoped the floor was solid. There were 14 kingfisher holes in the wall, evidence

Another aspect of Red-backed Kingfisher country near Mt Isa.

of long occupation even allowing for two holes in some years. The birds are intensely territorial, guaranteeing that only one pair would have used the site in any one season.

This was the only nest where we were certain that the birds had laid. The pile of fine dust below an entrance directed us to the right hole and, probing gently with a fine twig, I could feel the rounded contours of at least two eggs at the end of a 45-centimetre tunnel.

By the last week in September it was clear that we were not going to find any kingfishers with young and that I would have to work with a nest at an earlier stage. I chose one in a road cutting where the birds were still excavating.

There is a perception that inland Australia is always hot but that first morning was dry and clear with a bitingly cold wind. There was not a sign of a kingfisher but this was typical of a bird that can switch in an instant from showy exhibitionist to total recluse. It was an hour before that switch was reversed and I heard the familiar piping call.

It was not hard to see him, perched conspicuously at the top of a tree, the sun glinting off the metallic blue of his wings. The breeze lifted his bristly crest and he let out a long rattling call. I had heard similar calls from the Sacred Kingfisher and knew that he would soon be coming to the nest. He landed on a dead twig in front of the bank, stopping to check the safety both of the surroundings and of the hole itself.

There were three holes in the bank, two of them looking newly dug. A huge amount of effort goes into digging these holes and I was puzzled over why so many were abandoned in favour of what often appeared to be an identical site. The kingfisher paused, gave a low musical trill, then a frog-like croak and launched himself at the higher of the two holes, flying straight into the narrow entrance and appearing not even to touch the sides. For a few moments his tail remained visible and then he disappeared from view, remaining inside for more than a minute.

When he emerged, he came out backwards, proof that the chamber was incomplete and that there was still not enough room to turn around. He flew to the same perch, rested for a moment and was then

Red-backed Kingfishers may use a favoured nesting area for many years. This abandoned copper mine shows the remains of 13 holes of varying ages.

back in for another dig. This was a limestone wall, sandwiched with layers of a black mica-like substance, and very hard. It was certainly hard for the kingfishers, and the tailings below the entrance were a fine, black grit that might have come off a grindstone. I looked at the bills of both birds and they had lost their typical dagger points, becoming rounded and noticeably shortened. Why they would choose to tunnel in such rocky spots is hard to say for there were other places where the ground was clearly softer but every pair we found had chosen a site that would have tested a man with a hammer and chisel.

The male flew away for an hour and when he returned the female came with him. She was a duller bird than him and had a shorter crest but was still very striking. He was the first to fly to the hole to dig and she waited for him to come out. Then, when she went in, he could not curb his impatience and followed her so that both birds were working inside together. Twice they perched one above the other near the hole but I never saw them both together there again.

Digging in this ground is a slow process. I first saw this nest hole on 23 September. Eight days later, when we were ready to leave, the tunnel went in for 45 centimetres but there were still no eggs: a huge expenditure of effort before the real business of breeding had even begun.

With no feeding taking place at the nest, it was difficult to know what the kingfishers were eating. Skinks were plentiful everywhere and, with locust swarms starting to build, there was certainly ample prey available.

This place seemed so ideally suited, I found myself wondering how the kingfishers had fared before the advent of mining. Ideal it might be, but a considerable feature was the artificial nest sites and there seemed to be very few natural alternatives. Nowadays, the Red-backed Kingfishers seem as much a part of the landscape as the Wedge-tailed Eagles and the Grasswrens but it may not always have been so.

Two years later, I returned. It had been a season of abundant rain. The spinifex was greener than I had ever seen it and there were wildflowers in profusion but water cannot lie on this porous land and the ground seemed as dry as ever. As for the kingfishers, we found even more breeding than before. Every mine shaft, dry gully, creek bank and road cutting seemed to have a pair and the 13 nests we found were certainly only a small proportion of the total. The time of year was almost the

Left: The author inspects four nest holes in a creek bank. Red-backed Kingfishers usually, or possibly always, use a tunnel only once. Below: John Young looks into an old mine where the kingfishers nest.

same but breeding appeared to be more advanced than in 1995. All pairs were at the same stage of incubating eggs but there was no sign of any having hatched.

The tunnels in the creek banks were in sand and clay, a much softer medium than the rocky mine shafts, and it was perhaps significant that we found several of these had been dug out by goannas. Perhaps so many birds choose the rocky walls of the mine shafts for protection against one of their deadliest predators, with the creek banks being occupied only in the years of most prolific breeding.

Unfortunately, I could not stay to see any of the young hatch, leaving that stage of my Red-backed Kingfisher studies unfinished.

CHAPTER SEVEN
SACRED KINGFISHER

Halcyon sancta! The Sacred Kingfisher! It does not need a knowledge of Latin to detect the mystique in the old scientific name. The Sacred is one of four Australian and 39 kingfishers worldwide that were long classified as all belonging to a single genus, *Halcyon*. This classification and naming of kingfishers is a fascinating subject, even for the non-taxonomist. The generic names *Halcyon, Ceyx, Alcedo* and *Ceryle* all have their origins in Greek and Roman times. In Greek mythology, Halcyon was the daughter of the wind god, Aeolus, and threw herself into the sea out of devotion to her shipwrecked husband Ceyx. Both were transformed into kingfishers and nested on the surface of the sea, which had been purposely made calm by Aeolus, hence 'halcyon days'.

Halcyon was, until recently, the generic name for the Sacred, Forest, Collared and Red-backed Kingfishers while *Ceyx* covered the Little and the Azure. *Ceyx* is now used only for Dwarf and Pygmy Kingfishers and the two Australian *Ceyx* have been moved into *Alcedo*, a Latin word that, not surprisingly, means kingfisher. *Dacelo*, the kookaburra genus, is an anagram of *Alcedo*, as is *Lacedo*, the generic name for the Banded Kingfisher of South-East Asia. Finally, *Ceryle*, from the Latin for blue, is the generic name for the Pied Kingfisher of Africa and Asia, paradoxically one of the few kingfishers in the world that does not have blue in its plumage.

Taxonomists have a penchant for changing names and their moves can be quite bewildering. Under the conventions governing scientific naming, the Australian *Halcyons* have now been given their own genus of *Todiramphus*. I have no idea of the derivation but it is a cumbersome word and it seems a pity to lose the mythical *Halcyon*. Fortunately, it does nothing to detract from the colour and fascinating qualities of the birds themselves, which live in complete ignorance of what we are calling them.

Australia is rich in kingfishers and the 10 breeding species have evolved to occupy a huge range of habitats. Some kingfishers are found along rivers, other kingfishers live in deserts. Rainforests are home to a specially adapted kingfisher, as are monsoon woodlands and tropical woodlands. Certain species need banks to nest, others need tree hollows, while some must find termite mounds, on the ground for some species, in trees for others.

Some species are highly specific in their requirements. Others are more catholic and are prepared to use a variety of nest sites. Such a bird is the Sacred Kingfisher, the dry-land kingfisher of the temperate woodlands.

A male Sacred Kingfisher arrives at the nest with a
green grasshopper (left) and then a dragonfly (right).

A Victorian woodland in September. It is early morning and the air is filled with birdsong:
whistlers, thrushes, tree-creepers, Willy Wagtails, robins. All of these are present throughout the year but this morning these voices are joined by those of the new arrivals, the
spring migrants. The clear, descending trills of Fan-tailed Cuckoos carry through the rolling
calls of Olive-backed Orioles. There are the sounds of Leaden Flycatchers and Rufous
Fantails, and then there is the voice of the Sacred Kingfisher.

The call of the Sacred Kingfisher is one of the sounds of spring in southern Australia, a sharp,
penetrating "Kik kik kik, Kik kik kik", delivered with such verve it is often quite clearly audible from
half a kilometre away. Each triplet lasts for just over a second but is repeated almost as often, so a
bird may call 15 or more times a minute.

This is the call of the male, newly arrived and letting the world know he has claimed a territory
and is on the lookout for a mate. Interestingly, these strident calls are probably the first sounds he

Flying from the nest, the male Sacred Kingfisher reveals his full beauty.

A Sacred Kingfisher on the way to the nest with prey.

has made in the past eight months, for Sacred Kingfishers are almost completely silent outside the breeding season. The males are always the first to arrive and their calling is as much an enticement to an unattached female as it is a proclamation of ownership of a territory. It is not difficult to know when that female has appeared. The territorial calls become interspersed with harsh, protracted screams, certainly given by the female but possibly by the male also.

As these calls came I knew it was time to start looking for a nest. There is a technique to this. The screams are made by birds of a pair engaged in establishing their bond, but they are also given just as a bird is flying to the nest hole, greatly facilitating the search. I traced the source of the call, moving slowly to avoid disturbance. Then the scream came again and I watched her launch herself from a dead limb, flailing across a small clearing to hit the trunk of a mahogany tree with a short cry of "Tac". She had landed at the beginnings of a small knothole but it was not all that long since the branch had fallen away and there was no hole. She pecked at the wood but it was hard and her bill made no impression. She took off but only back to the same perch as a launching place to come back and try again, flying at the tree with a chattering call and then the same sharp cry of "Tac" as she hit the trunk.

As he comes in to land, the flight feathers of the male Sacred Kingfisher curl back with the pressure of air.

With wings, head and tail all on the same plane, the female's approach to the nest differs from the male's.

I have seen Sacred Kingfishers do this as a distraction display when there is a rival bird nearby, flying noisily and repeatedly to a fictitious nest when they already have an established site. On this day, however, it was a genuine effort to find a nest site in an area of bush where I had not seen Sacreds nesting before. For an hour she attempted to breach the tree and was still trying when I walked away. Possibly there were no good sites there at all for there was no sign of kingfishers the next time I went back and I never heard them calling there again.

In the northern part of their range many Sacred Kingfishers nest in termite mounds, and in some other regions they mostly nest in earthen banks, but in south-east Victoria they seem to use tree hollows exclusively.

Sacred Kingfishers that nest in termite mounds or banks must excavate their own holes but I doubt if those that use tree hollows ever do, although they may clean out some of the soft, rotten wood inside

Leaving the nest, the Sacred Kingfisher
flies straight towards the camera.

The camera captures movements that are too fast for the human eye to notice. Springing away from the nest, the Sacred Kingfisher is here shown briefly flying completely upside down.

the hole. There is clearly an optimum size and I have been repeatedly surprised at how they can squeeze through tiny knotholes into an interior that is usually only slightly more spacious.

There is obvious survival value in choosing a hollow with the smallest possible entrance so as to exclude competitors and predators. Such sites are highly desirable and may be used year after year. My personal experience is limited but I have known one hollow that has been used for at least five consecutive years up to the present. Of course, there is no such thing as the completely invulnerable site. One hollow was used for two years and then feral bees took over an adjacent hole, barely a metre away. The kingfishers still attempted to nest and got as far as hatching but they always seemed nervous and the young were abandoned. Possibly it was simply too hazardous to keep running the gauntlet of bees.

Even a tiny hole is not a certain defence against the rapacious goanna. I watched one climbing to a kingfisher hole 10 metres above the ground in the trunk of a eucalypt. Throughout the climb, the frantic kingfishers attacked repeatedly, diving at it with piercing screams and striking it with their bills. Totally unperturbed, the goanna climbed inexorably upwards towards the doomed nestlings. It took only moments to enlarge the opening with its steely claws and the young were gone. I am only amazed that this does not happen more often. Kingfishers in general do little to disguise their nest sites. The young are noisy, the nests are smelly, the ground below the entrance becomes covered with excreta while the adults have loud and characteristic calls as they approach with food. If anything is going to attract a goanna, then surely all of this will.

The 1993 nest did not suffer such a fate. I found it on 10 January, my attention drawn by the repeated loud screams as the adults approached the nest. I was only just in time, for the young flew six days later. Ten metres up in the trunk of a grey box tree, the hole's lower lip was made conspicuous by the white excreta that, lava-like, flowed out of the entrance. As though this were not enough to advertise their whereabouts, the young were never silent, calling constantly with a strange rhythmic, buzzing noise that sounded as though it were made under water. With their strong voices and the copious amount of whitewash, I felt they were probably close to flying. It took two days to work the hide into the best position and, on 14 January, I had my first session.

Sacred Kingfishers may be only small but they are audacious in defence of their young and, as I climbed to the hide, I was subjected to a series of screaming dives, not coming close enough to hit me but making it quite plain that my presence was not welcome. I barely had time to close the hide before the adults were trying to come back to the nest. Understandably, they were nervous, aborting their first few approach flights when only centimetres from the hole. Then the male landed but only momentarily and he was away again without passing over the food. The young called constantly, pushing their beaks out of the entrance in their eagerness to be fed. From their size and the colouring of their feathers, I could see that they were nearly ready to go.

The next time the male landed, he stayed long enough for a chick to grab the food. A few minutes later, the female did the same and, after that, both adults behaved as though I was not there. It was early afternoon, normally a time of little activity but, in two and a half hours, the kingfishers came in 38 times with food, a frequency of one visit every four minutes. Much of the prey was small: spiders, grasshoppers and other invertebrates. There were, however, also numerous skinks and I marvelled at a skill that enabled the kingfishers to seek out, capture and deliver prey at such a sustained rate. Presumably, this had been going on since soon after dawn and, even allowing for a slack period in the middle of the day, it seems likely that the kingfishers were visiting the nest at least 150 times per day. None of the visits lasted long. It took only a moment for the chick to snatch the food and the adult was gone, never stopping to enter the nest.

That was my only full session in the hide. When I arrived the next morning, one chick had its complete head looking out of the hole. It withdrew as I entered the hide but only for a moment and then the head appeared again, there was a heave of the shoulders and it was through and away, fluttering remarkably strongly to a nearby tree where it made its maiden landing.

The adults were very noisy and I felt they were trying to entice out the remaining young. There were territorial calls, short rising trills, the alarm shriek and a rasping noise that sounded very like the call of the White-naped Honeyeater. They continued to bring food to the hole but it was clearly a time for change and I knew that this would soon come.

After an hour a second chick appeared at the hole, gave a wriggle and was gone. Still the parents continued to bring in food, but not for long. Ten minutes later, a third young followed and the hollow became silent.

How long the young remain dependent on their parents, I cannot say. The next day, they were all still close to the nest tree but that was the last time I saw them. Other broods I have known have been equally quick to disperse but I have no idea whether or not they move away as a complete family.

I was keen to be able to show the Sacred Kingfisher's full beauty by photographing it in flight. The 1994 nest seemed ideal, only four metres up in the trunk of a Southern Mahogany and in a secluded area where I could safely leave my gear unattended. These kingfishers were to photograph themselves with the aid of the infra-red beam and, with no need for a hide, I attached the camera and flashes in the tree, little more than a metre from the entrance. After a brief period of suspicion, the adults treated all these additions to their surroundings as though they had always been there and continued in similar vein when I finally switched on the equipment.

The birds behaved perfectly but such camera techniques need adjusting and, when the young flew on the last day of December, I was still not happy with my results. On the day before they flew, I climbed to the hole to have a look. So cramped was the cavity that I was unable to count the tightly packed chicks but I had no difficulty in seeing the heaving mass of maggots on the foul-smelling floor of the hollow. Nest hygiene is clearly not a feature of kingfisher life.

Open forest, in eastern Victoria, home of the Sacred Kingfisher.

The next year, I was too late. Coming to inspect the site on 14 December, I found a flying chick noisily following its parent. This was more than a fortnight earlier than in 1994.

So to 1996 and it seemed that I would again be unsuccessful. I arrived on 19 November and the birds were certainly there. However, they were behaving strangely, neither incubating nor feeding young but flying repeatedly to the nest, giving a sharp call of "Chack" and flying off again. They seemed agitated and with good cause: I climbed to the hole and found three chicks, newly hatched but all dead. For the previous two days, there had been cold, driving rain from the south-west and with the entrance of the hole facing that way, it seems that the young may have succumbed to the weather.

It looked as though the season would be a failure but something made me go back for another look in late December. To my surprise, the female flew from the same hole and, a few days later, it was clear that there were already young. This time I was able to count them, five, which hatched, I think, on 26 December, only 37 days after I had found the first brood dead. With incubation reported at 18 days, the second clutch must have been started little more than a fortnight after the first young had died.

This time, I took some pictures using the light beam but also spent time in the hide. There were some surprises. Sacred Kingfishers are only small birds but much of their prey was considerably bigger than that brought in by the Laughing Kookaburras I had been watching a few weeks before. Skinks were caught in profusion but more surprising was a small bird, probably a nestling, and also a mouse, an item I had certainly not expected. I had thought the 15 visits per hour remarkable at the 1994 nest but that was almost pedestrian against this pair which, on their most prolific morning, came to the nest with food 26 times in less than an hour.

Photographically I also did better and not only was this pleasing but it also brought surprises, the most notable being the picture of a kingfisher flying completely upside down as it threw itself away from the nest tree.

After the earlier failure, I was glad to see these young get away successfully and they flew on 26 January, more than six weeks later than the previous year's brood. As is usual, they dispersed quickly and I did not see them again.

CHAPTER EIGHT
COLLARED KINGFISHER

The Collared Kingfisher! Lord of the mangroves! Mangroves are rich in birds of many groups, many of them with distinctive songs and calls; but if Collared Kingfishers are in residence their presence overshadows all others.

This is their domain, a fact quickly impressed upon anybody who happens to venture into Collared Kingfisher territory. "Kik kik kik, Kik kik kik." The calls ring out at once: loud, strident and aggressive. A proclamation of ownership that nobody could fail to recognise.

At Portland Roads, high up on Cape York Peninsula, is a forest of the tallest mangroves I have ever seen. The trees are 30 metres high, their trunks unbranched between the tangled chaos of their tide-washed roots and the dark canopy above. They are widely spaced, allowing almost unhindered vision through the forest, but so dense is the canopy's umbrella that it produces a zone of perpetual twilight. This creates a problem for human eyes and for cameras but not, it seems, for Collared Kingfishers.

I had not even entered the mangroves when the first one saw me and began to challenge my right to be there. The cry was quickly taken up by its neighbours to my left, to my right and also deeper into the forest. In the dim light it was not easy to spot them, even with the benefit of the repeated calling. Then one flew, a striking and powerful kingfisher with a huge dagger beak. In this light it appeared to be black and white and it would need sunlight to bring out the iridescent blues and greens of the plumage.

I tried to follow them, dragging my 600mm lens and tripod through mud and tide and across the impossible maze of aerial roots. It was a hopeless task, hazardous to both legs and cameras and bringing me only as close as the kingfishers would allow before they sailed away through the forest. It was November, close to the start of the wet season and they seemed particularly noisy in defence of their territories. I looked for termite mounds on the sides of the mangrove trunks but there seemed to be very few. One bird flew several times to a hole in the trunk of a mangrove but appeared unable to squeeze inside. Even these huge mangroves appeared unlikely to have many hollows big enough to accommodate this very large kingfisher. Such hollows would have to be discovered at a different place altogether.

Mangroves at Innisfail where Collared Kingfishers live. Although difficult, access is slightly easier than at Portland Roads.

The Collared Kingfisher was long known as the Mangrove Kingfisher and, in Australia, the name was particularly apt. In other parts of the world, the many races of this species occupy a wide variety of habitats but in Australia it is almost exclusively a bird of mangroves, occurring across the top of the country from northern New South Wales in the east to the central coast of Western Australia. Its distribution is uneven, partly following that of the mangroves, although not all of the mangrove areas are occupied by Collared Kingfishers.

My search for these birds brought me south from Cape York to Innisfail in north Queensland. There I was greatly helped by Jim Browning, a professional prawn fisherman who had long been fascinated by the kingfishers around the tidal creeks where he worked.

In 1994 he found a pair nesting in a big termite mound attached to an acacia, right at the edge of the mangroves and above the high-tide mark. There was an elkhorn fern above the mound, making it a very picturesque site with the added advantage to me of being able to stand my tower on dry ground. Here I planned to start my study.

I had my first session in the hide on 19 October. If the birds at Portland Roads had been noisy, the adults here were positively frenetic. As we entered the forest, both adults appeared, their sharp "Kikik" calls loud and aggressive, running into a staccato "Kee kee, Kee kee, Kee kee" with the second call higher than the first. I settled down to wait and the kingfishers settled to some extent, too, but it was soon clear they were trying to entice the young to leave the nest. They brought no

Above: Collared Kingfisher country at Portland Roads, an almost impenetrable tangle of mangrove roots. Opposite: an adult at the nest. Note the extremely powerful bill.

food but repeatedly approached close, uttering harsh trills and chuckles not unlike those of the Sacred Kingfisher's but louder.

After an hour they succeeded. There was a whirring sound and I had a glimpse of an almost tailless baby kingfisher disappearing among the trees, stubby wings working furiously. Two hours later a second chick followed. That was the complete brood and there was nothing to be gained by staying longer in the hide. I searched the area and found one of the babies perched close to the ground. It was well able to fly and its parents called to it constantly. I did not see it again.

The next year, Jim excelled himself, detecting 13 pairs of birds and six active nests. To have such a selection was an unexpected luxury but the choice was not quite as wide as it seemed. One of the nests was in the termite mound where I had watched the young leave last season and, two days before I arrived, the same thing happened again. It was almost exactly the same date so the birds were at least consistent.

That left five, but four of them were far out in the tidal mangroves, which were much more closely packed than at Portland Roads. I could have worked on them but it would have been wet, muddy and difficult.

Fortunately, I did not have to make that choice. The sixth pair was hunting in the mangroves but was not nesting there at all, flying out to the edge of a small clearing where there was an electricity pole with three large termite mounds on the side. Two of them bore the crumbling scars of old kingfisher holes, but in the third there was the clean, circular entrance to a new nest, broken away a little on the lower lip where the adults had been perching. From across the clearing came the

Collared Kingfisher at the nest. Note the green ants, which sometimes invaded the nest in thousands.

In full flight, the Collared Kingfisher reveals the rich blue of its wings and tail.

Short beak and short tail. A baby Collared Kingfisher just after its maiden flight.

familiar aggressive cry "Kik kik kik, Kik kik kik". Both birds were at the top of a dead tree, voicing displeasure at their unwelcome visitor. I moved back 50 metres and waited.

It did not take long. Within minutes, one of the kingfishers flew across and landed on a power-line running from the top of the pole. It was carrying prey: a black crustacean that looked like a small crayfish. From there the bird took one swoop and it was at the nest, plunging down steeply to a level below the hole and then slowing sharply as it lifted up to the entrance over the last few metres. As it landed, its bill was already in the hole and in an instant the crayfish was gone, drawn into the nest cavity as though by an invisible hand. The adult, which had made no attempt to go inside, dropped away and was gone.

Despite this show of strength, I felt that the young were probably still very small. From the hide, little more than two metres away, I could barely hear their calls and they had not yet started to squirt their excreta out of the entrance. However, the worn and broken lower lip of the hole was evidence of many landings and I had been caught out by young kingfishers before. For the next few days, I would spend as much time as possible in the hide.

Kingfishers tend not to be early starters and I left my arrival until two hours after sunrise to be greeted by both birds in their usual vociferous fashion. It was a statement of ownership, not of fear, and I was scarcely in the hide when the female came to the nest. She heralded her approach with a short "Kakakak" followed by a soft trill and then she was at the hole, thrusting the crayfish forward for the bills of the waiting young. Moments later, the male followed her in. His colours were brighter than hers and, although the overall plumage was very similar, it was always easy to tell the two birds apart.

In the first three hours, there were 14 visits to the nest, eight by the female and six by the male. Mostly, the prey was crayfish but there were also two green grasshoppers and a small crab, already stripped of its legs.

At 11 a.m., after three hours of bringing food, the male gave a particularly sharp "Kakak" and flew at the mound to strike it with his beak and fly straight off. Moments later, he did the same again and then again and again. I had previously noticed a long column of green ants ascending the tree and into the hole. Some of them were coming back out carrying blowfly maggots but there seemed to be far more going in than coming out. Now I realised that these were the objects of the king-fisher's strikes and he was flicking them off the mound with his bill each time he landed. In just over half an hour, he made 52 visits, by which time there were very few ants to be seen. It would be only a brief respite, for the supply of ants was countless.

At this point the female arrived with food again and the spell was broken. In a quarter of an hour the pair brought prey eight times, an indication of their remarkable hunting prowess.

The afternoon session was less prolific. By now the tide was up and with very little mud left exposed the kingfishers brought food only four times. I had noticed before how Collared Kingfishers tend to move to the main channels as the tide comes in and their hunting opportunities are obviously curtailed by the rising water.

By my third day, the calls of the young were noticeably stronger and I could see the black tips of their bills as they waited for their parents to return. There was colour in their head feathers and they were clearly growing very fast, no surprise in view of the quantity of food their parents were pack-ing into them.

On that morning, a third kingfisher landed in the territory, producing an immediate but unex-pected reaction from the two owners. Both the resident birds started by calling sharply with tails cocked high in the air but then, instead of pursuing the intruder, they began to attack last season's nest mound, which was higher up the pole, striking it with rattling cries and sending clods of dried

mud flying. It was a strange display but it had its effect and the newcomer left as rapidly as it had come. Perhaps it was intended to show the occupants' potential in attack; it certainly saved injury on both sides.

I had only four days to spend with these birds and left with the young still in the nest and not knowing when they would leave. Fortunately, Jim was able to keep regular watch and it was 13 days after I left before they took their first flight. This was a surprise to me as I had thought them within a few days of leaving when I finished my stay there.

A surprise, too, was the speed with which the adults began their next brood and 15 days after the young flew the female was back in the same hole incubating her next clutch. I was not only surprised but puzzled too. The birds had raised two young only but were now putting themselves through another enormous expenditure of time and energy to produce a further brood. Food had appeared easy to obtain during the previous brood and some other kingfishers produce three, four or even five young. Why not these? It was certainly not an isolated habit for one of Jim's other pairs did the same thing. There are many unexplained happenings in the natural world and it seems that, for the time being, this must remain one of them.

Collared Kingfisher
on the way to its nest
with a crab. Crabs and
crayfish make up the
majority of the prey.

CHAPTER NINE
YELLOW-BILLED KINGFISHER

Cape York! One of the great wildernesses of Australia. It is 1970 and my first visit to Iron Range near its northern tip. Walking along the track, the forest beside me seems an uncharted jungle: dense, dark, almost impenetrable and seemingly without landmarks, a place where one could become lost within metres of venturing inside. I strain my eyes to peer into the fringing thicket but see nothing and then, right beside my head, comes the sound, a piercing, rattling, downscale trill, so close that it is almost painful to the eardrums. I look even harder but see only green leaves and darkness. Finally, there is a slight movement and I am able to spot the vocalist, a small vivid green and gold kingfisher with a bright yellow bill. Despite the intensity of his colours, I would never have seen him had he not called. This is the Yellow-billed Kingfisher, the only one I shall see on this visit but a sight that leaves an indelible impression.

The Yellow-billed Kingfisher is not the easiest of birds to study. It occurs only around the northern tip of Cape York Peninsula, a remote and inaccessible region that is always going to have a much greater density of birds than of birdwatchers.

Its breeding is timed to coincide with the start of the wet season, a variable phenomenon that may begin any time from mid-October to early January or, in some years, not begin at all.

In December 1987 and again in October 1988, I was there in search of owls. On both occasions, I camped in sodden forest and looked for the owls between tropical storms. There was no doubt that the wet season had started and, although I was not looking for kingfishers, the calls of the Yellow-bills and the sight of freshly dug nest holes were clear evidence that breeding had begun.

With the dates of these sightings in mind, I returned with John Young in the last week of November 1993, this time with the kingfisher as my quarry. It was a long journey, two days' drive

Opposite: Crown feathers raised, this male Yellow-billed Kingfisher appears in all his beauty. The size of the black eye is enhanced by the black ring around it.

from Cairns on bone-jarring roads where speed is impossible. I hoped that the timing was correct, for we had no means of finding out beforehand.

We nearly got it right. Three weeks later would have found breeding in full swing but the dry season had been a long one, holding back the start of nesting for many species. The forest was dry in a way I had never seen here before. Leaves crackled underfoot, parched foliage hung limply from the trees, and by mid-morning the forest seemed gripped by torpor, the air hot and still, the birds silent. Nevertheless, there was a rousing dawn chorus on our first morning and it was clear that the birds were all here, waiting. All that was needed was rain.

A walk through the forest confirmed our suspicions. Yellow-billed Kingfishers nest in the rounded arboreal mounds of termites of the genus *Eutermes*, usually in open woodland near the rainforest edge. There was no lack of mounds but they were not being used and there was no sign anywhere of a bird. We looked too at the conical, black, terrestrial mounds, favoured by the Buff-breasted Paradise-Kingfisher. By now the birds should certainly have returned from their dry-season migration to New Guinea, but if they were in the area it was certainly not obvious.

On the second night it rained, the heavy rain of the tropics. The towering clouds came with rolling thunder and sheet upon sheet of brilliant lightning. The storm itself was short but furious, and in the morning, a change had come over the land. The air was filled with the scents of warm earth and wet leaves, insects had appeared in profusion and the birds had come to life.

Reconnaissance the day before had turned up several likely nest sites and we did not have to go far. Twenty minutes' walk from camp the first mound, the size of a soccer ball and almost spherical, was wedged in a low fork of a tree. Typical of this genus of termite, the surface was uniformly pitted in a fine honeycomb pattern. The previous day this pattern had been unblemished but since then, at the equator of the mound, a few small chips had been broken away. This was the work of a Yellow-billed Kingfisher.

The following day I arrived near the mound soon after dawn. There had been more rain overnight but now it was clear and still. For an hour I heard nothing but then, faintly and in the distance, came the trill of a Yellow-billed. It came again and then a third time, always from the same direction and a long way off. Then silence. I had almost given up hope when I was startled by the male's rich trill, only metres away. The female answered, her trill less musical and a little deeper than his. They were both close to the mound, she on a dead stick almost level with it and only three metres away. She trilled again, an all-consuming call, tail cocked and quivering, bill raised to the sky and throat pulsing with the outpouring of her passion.

She turned to face the mound and her demeanour changed. She called, a harsh "Chack chack chack", cocked her tail once and flew straight at the mound, hitting it with her bill with such force that she literally bounced off. The impact on brain and neck must have been enormous. She returned to the stick and repeated the performance a second and then a third time. I thought the male would do the same but, when he flew, it was to land momentarily on her back. Then they both left. The female's efforts had produced a little more chipping on the termite mound but a nest hole was still a long way off. For the time being, the rain had gone and, with its passing, the kingfishers' enthusiasm also waned. I needed to look elsewhere.

A few minutes' walk away, I watched a female begin digging. She had probably only just begun, for the mound looked pristine and, as the first chips flew, the termites came pouring out through the breach in their defences. She did not continue there and it would seem that many species of king-fisher may start digging several nest holes before going on to complete one or, as sometimes happens, abandoning them all.

Caught in a beam of sunlight, the Yellow-billed Kingfisher's head glows with gold.

All was not yet lost. On 4 December, John found a new mound with the hole already dug. The female flew out as he approached and this was clearly the most promising find yet. Attached to a short dead limb on a small bloodwood, this was the most perfectly shaped mound I had yet seen: an almost complete sphere with the entrance hole right on its equator. I spent almost four days at this nest but, finally, time caught up with me and I left with most of my Yellow-billed Kingfisher questions still unanswered.

There was no doubt that this was an active nest and the male made it quite plain that he was the owner but, throughout this time, I never caught a glimpse of the female. Perhaps she was inside and incubating but, if so, it is strange that she never flew out and was not fed there by the male. Possibly the inside of a tropical termite mound is a natural incubator, removing the need for the birds to sit

Trilling male. The call is delivered with an all-consuming passion.

on the eggs at all, at least by day. Once only the male flew to the mound and looked inside but there seemed no more purpose in his visit than to check that all was well.

He was quite unconcerned about my presence and I sat on an open platform, sometimes with him perched only two or three metres away, a privilege in itself. All kingfishers are beautiful but there is something quite exquisite about the Yellow-billed. The deep orange head feathers glow like the sunset, looking particularly beautiful when puffed out and with the bristly crest raised. The eyes are dramatic and unexpected, jet black in colour and huge in size, an adaptation to hunting in the dim light of the rainforest. The deep yellow bill has an almost translucent quality and, below it, the

In full voice. With bill raised and cocked tail quivering, a female Yellow-billed Kingfisher pours out her trill.

orange of the head continues onto the breast, fading gradually to pale yellow on the belly. The wings are dark green and the tail blue while the deep yellow appears again on the feet.

The wet season was gradually setting in and my vigils at the nest were punctuated by the daily storms, which appeared almost without warning. The brilliance of day would drop away to a stygian gloom and kingfishers were temporarily forgotten in my efforts to protect my equipment from the torrents of rain. Every leaf ran a small river and, drenched with water, the top half of the nest mound darkened to a deep chocolate black. The humidity inside must have been intense.

Iron Range is 700 kilometres up Cape York, a wonderful place to visit but one where it is also very easy to get stuck. The wet season is not a time to be lingering there and another day's delay could mean being held up for weeks. We headed south while we still could.

It was another two years before I could try again. We went just one week later than in 1993. Such are the vagaries of the tropical wet season that we were almost too late.

There is only one road up Cape York and it is very vulnerable, unsealed for most of the way and traversing numerous riverbeds that can be dry one day and impassable the next. It was 1 December when we started and the signs were not good. We ran into a huge storm and before long it seemed the whole countryside was awash. There was still traffic on the road but it differed from us in one major respect: it was all travelling south. We were going north and we were alone. At Laura, a third of the way up the Cape, the causeway was still dry when we crossed. The following morning, the water was three metres deep and it was 10 days before the road was open again. We had been lucky.

Silver Plains, on the east side of Cape York, is not as far north as Iron Range. It marks the southerly limit of the Yellow-billed Kingfisher's range and was new country for me. The rainforest exists in strips along the Rocky and Massy rivers and their tributaries. It is a place of great beauty with lush rainforest arching over narrow, fast-flowing streams. Most of the northern Cape York birds are here and it was a dramatic sight to see the huge Palm Cockatoos lift off from a drinking spot and weave their way along the narrow corridor between river and forest.

Our visit here was a gamble. We had come a long way and had it only on repute that the Yellow-billed Kingfisher was here at all. Within an hour of arriving, we had settled that question with one bird trilling near our camp site and two more within half a kilometre. By nightfall we had two nests and were feeling rather pleased with ourselves. We were premature.

The next morning revealed that one mound was totally unsuitable for photography, 30 metres up near the top of one of the highest trees in the forest. The second nest, low down and accessible,

A typical Yellow-billed Kingfisher nest in an arboreal termite mound. The entrance hole is near the base of the mound.

The male Yellow-billed Kingfisher delivers a small reptile to the nest.

seemed perfect but, on going there, we were met by two flying young that had clearly left the nest that morning. We began again.

Two hours later, we watched from the side slopes of a gully as a male Yellow-bill carried food to a nest and fed the young. The site was perfect, a domed mound only 10 metres from the ground in a bloodwood tree where the forest was quite open. Surely the young here would not leave before we had a chance to spend some time with them?

We began the hide at once, siting it in an adjacent tree and level with the nest. I cut the poles while John did the building under a constant bombardment from the kingfishers. There was nothing timid about these little birds, which attacked him as ferociously as any falcon, hitting him repeatedly on the head and even diving in below the brim of his hat. With the building completed, we left and they were back feeding the young within minutes.

The next morning I began my first session. There was no sign of an adult but a soft and constant sound of "Chewchewchew" from within the mound told me all was well with the young. Within minutes I heard a rattling "Chak-ak-ak" and the male was there, perched on a horizontal limb level with the nest. From the amount of wear on the bark, this was the regular approach point to the nest. He carried an insect in his bill and, ignoring me completely, flew quickly to the nest, perching on the outside and proferring the prey through the hole, where it was seized and drawn inside.

Five minutes later the call came again and it was the female, carrying a sizeable gecko. Her plumage was similar to the male but duller and with a large black patch on the crown and a smaller

Above: The chick perched and looked back after its first flight. Note the short bill and the bluish ring around the eye. Below: Front view of the same young chick.

one on each side of the neck. She flew to the nest and the much larger prey was drawn inside with equal ease. Clearly, the young were already well grown.

In the next five hours, there were nine more visits, four by the male and five by the female. Altogether, they brought five skinks, one gecko and four large but unidentified insects. Interestingly, this prey is bigger than most of that taken by the much larger Buff-breasted Paradise-Kingfisher or even by kookaburras.

After feeding, the adult usually flew back to the approach tree to rest and often to sing. To see a male give his trill is to see an avian diva in full voice. The bill is wide open, the head thrown sky-wards, the tail cocked up with the whole tail and body quivering with the effort of the performance. The first few trills usually last two to three seconds but there are often several, leading to the final prolonged fortissimo that can last for as long as eight seconds in a performance that would be the envy of any coloratura soprano. This long trill is always followed by a rest but the call is often taken up by the bird's mate or by a neighbour so that a bout of calling may go on for some time.

The next morning I was back in the hide again early. My plan was to have two days of portrait photography before setting up the infra-red beam for flight pictures. It was not to be. For the first hour there were no surprises with both birds delivering a skink to the young. Then both adults landed in the approach tree and began trilling together.

I was too engrossed in them to watch the nest until a blur of green and blue feathers went past the hide and I looked round to see a baby Yellow-billed Kingfisher perched in the tree just behind me. It was much smaller than its parents with a short black beak, tiny stump of a tail, fleshy legs and blue instead of black patches on the nape. At once it started to preen and clouds of fine down drifted along the breeze towards me.

At this the behaviour of the adults changed and the female perched close to it, using the same soft "Chewchewchew" call I had heard from the young in the nest. For several minutes, the baby stayed there. Then the male flew past me, landed farther away in the forest and trilled, leaning forward as he did so. The chick copied him, leaning forward too, overbalanced and was away, whirring along for 20 metres before making a quite passable landing without so much as losing height.

Half an hour later, a second chick left the nest, making a temporary stop on the frame of the hide before moving on and landing near its sibling. There was great excitement among the parents with animated chattering and trilling and then the female arrived with a snake that was fully 15 centimetres long. She seemed not to realise the nest was empty and flew to it twice, looking hard and long inside before taking the prey and feeding it to one of the young. Later in the morning, the male caught another skink but by this time the family was moving away and was barely visible from the hide. When we returned the next day, they were nowhere to be found.

For the next three days, we searched the district. We saw numerous Yellow-billed Kingfishers but none visiting nests and concluded that all had completed their nesting. Whether or not that was correct, I shall never know but I am quite certain that, had I arrived just two days later, I would have had no success at all. I count myself very lucky.

CHAPTER TEN
BUFF-BREASTED
PARADISE-KINGFISHER

Deep in a north Queensland rainforest in November, amid the clamour of birds and frogs and insects, a new sound has appeared overnight: a soft, pulsing, yet penetrating "Cherwill cherwill cherwill cherwill". I have been here a week with no sign of this call but suddenly it is coming to me from all corners of the forest floor. The Buff-breasted Paradise-Kingfishers have arrived.

The return of the paradise-kingfishers is almost as spectacular as the birds themselves. They are wet-season visitors, spending the drier months of April to October in New Guinea before flooding back to Australia. Usually they seem to arrive at night and there are few, if any, pathfinders. I have never witnessed the migration but it seems that it is a mass arrival, filling every corner of the forest in one sudden influx.

There is an urgency about the calling, for these new arrivals are invaders, ready to start breeding at once and, with an oversupply of mature birds, there is an immediate need to establish a territory. It seems very likely that many birds return annually to the same piece of forest but not enough work has yet been done to prove this. Even though there appears to be an abundant choice of termite mounds for nest sites, the same ones are often used repeatedly, which seems to indicate a prior knowledge on the part of the occupants.

Among the many colourful kingfishers the Buff-breasted Paradise-Kingfisher is just about the showiest of all, with plumage that is quite astonishingly gaudy. It is a large kingfisher, brilliant iridescent royal blue above contrasting with bright orange below. The salmon-pink bill seems too big for the body and the tail, blue at its base, has two white central tail feathers, as long as the whole of the rest of the bird. These taper gradually until they cross just before the tips.

It is an extraordinary colour scheme and, with such brilliance, it is strange to find that the bird is quite hard to spot in the dim light of the rainforest. As with many kingfishers, however, it takes sunlight to ignite the colour and, in the shadowed gloom of the forest floor, the blues and reds lose their gleam and merge with the blacks and browns of dead leaves and tree trunks.

After feeding the young, a Buff-breasted Paradise-Kingfisher rests on a fallen log.

Seen at close quarters, the colours of the Buff-breasted Paradise-Kingfisher seem almost garish.

They are also shy birds, spotting an approaching human long before they are seen themselves and moving quietly from view so that it is from the cover of a hide that I have best been able to admire their extravagant beauty. For the females, the duties of incubation in a confined space usually bend the tail and frequently break it but the males are able to avoid these minor traumata and appear in their full glory.

The whole design of these birds seems to be directed to show rather than function but this appearance is deceptive. They manoeuvre remarkably well through the tangle of the rainforest and successfully undertake a migration which, for some of them, involves a sea crossing of at least 800 kilometres. Many birds must die at sea for they fly low to the water and arrive at the end of their journey in a state of severe exhaustion.

The Aborigines of the Bloomfield River district used to call these paradise-kingfishers "Tchewal-tchewal". It is an apt and onomatopoeic name, having the ring of the call of the newly arrived birds.

The perils of nesting in termite mounds on the ground. This Buff-breasted Paradise-Kingfisher nest has been dug out and robbed by a goanna.

The Lace Monitor or goanna, scourge of the Buff-breasted Paradise-Kingfisher and of many other birds and mammals.

It is a time of much noise and activity as they establish territories and choose their nest sites. Nobody yet seems to know if they have to find mates or are paired beforehand.

Usually, nest digging starts within a few days but, in dry conditions, this may be delayed for days or even weeks. I have seen many nests and all have been in small black termite mounds, usually on the ground but occasionally on a low stump or fallen log. These mounds are hard, yet still soft enough for the kingfishers to excavate with their bills, unlike some of the concrete-like structures of the nearby dry woodland.

Although the kingfishers appear to have a wide choice, the number of suitable mounds in each territory is probably quite small. Certainly, for the student of kingfishers, it does not take long to learn how to pick likely nests, making them relatively easy to find. Ornithologists are not the only ones looking for the nests, however, and goannas take a heavy toll of eggs and young.

These paradise-kingfishers are marvellous birds to study at the nest, readily accepting a hide with all its accompanying clicks and flashes. One nest mound was in a small forest glade, a stone's throw from the banks of a creek. It was a lush area of Black Bean, strangler figs, huge paperbarks and groves of elegant Liverstone palms. The wet season was late and the creek was reduced to a trickle, eight metres below the top of the bank. I never suspected that in little more than a week it would rise over 10 metres, inundating the forest and drowning all that could not move out of its way.

Even before I had my first session in the hide, it was possible to spot the birds' return path to the nest. A green, mossy log was rubbed clean in one spot while, closer to the nest, an exposed root was worn in a similar way.

I entered the hide and waited. It was a good hide and well camouflaged but there is always a time of nervousness when waiting for a new bird. They seem so shy in the forest and several of the other large kingfishers are very wary in front of a hide.

A bird called twice, at first some distance away but the second time much closer. Then from right behind me came a soft trill, descending the scale. To me, it did not sound agitated but I came to realise that this was a type of alarm call, used mostly when the birds had not completely settled down after my return to the hide. It was a call of nervousness rather than fear and, with young to feed, that nervousness was soon overcome. There was a flurry of wings and the scene was set alight as the female appeared on her regular approach log, carrying a large spider in her bill.

She saw the flash heads and was uncertain, waiting, watching for any sign of movement. It took two minutes and then she flew to the low root, only three metres from the nest mound and right below my hide. There she was at her most vulnerable and she waited again, fearful to make that last flight and reveal the whereabouts of her young.

Finally she launched herself but was still timid and banked away from the nest to land back on the log. The sequence was repeated. This time she made it to the nest hole but was away again

On the way to the nest, a male perches on a vine with an insect.

Male Buff-breasted Paradise-Kingfisher flying to the nest. When seen from above, the white tail is very conspicuous.

Above: Coming in flight to the nest, the male Buff-breasted Paradise-Kingfisher is a study in grace and form. Right: With head in the nest hole, the Buff-breasted Paradise-Kingfisher feeds her young. Females are readily recognisable as their tails always become bent or broken within the confines of the nest hole during incubation.

almost before she had hit it, still carrying the spider. That was enough to convince her. From then on she went back to the task of feeding her young, ignoring the hide, the camera and even the bursts of brilliant light from the flash heads. The male acted similarly but, with his mate already at ease, did not take as long to lose his fear and, within an hour of my entering the hide, they were both coming and going as though it did not exist.

For their size, paradise-kingfishers take very small prey, mainly insects, spiders, small skinks and tiny frogs. Once, at a different nest, I saw one come in with a tortoise but even this was a very small one. Most prey arrives in an unidentifiable state, limbs torn off by the mandatory beating all kingfishers administer to their catch. I am uncertain whether this serves to kill the prey or merely to make it more digestible but it sometimes has its disadvantages as I saw once when a spider flew to pieces with the ferocity of the onslaught, leaving nothing to feed to the young at all.

As the chicks grow larger, their presence becomes more and more obvious. Excreta and insect debris pile up below the entrance and the constant soft whirring calls of the young become gradually louder. The nest begins to smell, noticeable even to me and so surely also to the sensitive nostrils of the goannas. Nest defence is vital and the kingfishers perform this with great vigour.

A typical nest site in a terrestrial termite mound. The adults always have a favourite perch for the final flight to the nest.

This time the prey is a gecko. Buff-breasted
Paradise-Kingfishers catch a wide variety
of small reptiles, insects and arthropods.

Buff-breasted Paradise-Kingfisher

It is quiet at the nest. Both adults have been in recently with prey and I am not expecting another visit for some time. The fracas behind the hide starts without any warning: explosive screams with the sounds of wings thrashing through the bushes and the thump of body against body. This is only a small goanna and it is driven off, but episodes like this happen once or twice every day.

Not every defence is successful. John Young once watched a large goanna rip open a mound and eat the young. It took only a minute or two with the goanna ignoring the furious attacks of the adults which, although they dived and hit it repeatedly, were powerless, bouncing harmlessly off the armour-plated reptile's back.

Perched on a vine in the rainforest, the Buff-breasted Paradise-Kingfisher merges into its surroundings.

In 1994 I photographed two nesting pairs of paradise-kingfishers. Both accepted my hide readily but eventually both nests failed, engulfed by the flooding that heralded the start of the wet season. The following year I watched another nest, which was progressing well but, a week after I left, a goanna found it with the inevitable outcome. Fortunately, the fox has not yet reached this part of Australia and cats seem also to be relatively uncommon. Nevertheless, there are many barriers in the way of the kingfishers' attempts to raise their young.

Despite the hazards, by late January there are usually numbers of juvenile birds in the rainforest, perching high and calling repeatedly for food. With black bills, dull brown plumage and tails that are barely a third the length of the adults', they bear little resemblance to their brilliant parents.

They have little time to learn to look after themselves. By March, there are no longer any sounds of paradise-kingfishers in the forest and the adults have begun the migration back to New Guinea by themselves. Completely independent, the young stay on for a few weeks more before making the same journey, quite alone apart from other novice travellers of their own kind. How they, and many other migratory species, achieve this is a mystery that has long puzzled bird students and we seem to be no nearer the answer.

CHAPTER ELEVEN
PRACTICAL ASPECTS

Alll wildlife studies have their difficulties, but that is half the fun: the searching and climbing for raptors; the long waits in the darkness for owls. Compared with these, working with kingfishers was relatively problem-free but that does not mean it was easy.

> Standing waist-deep in a swampy lagoon, I watched a Taipan change direction and swim towards me. I froze, for in that medium I had no chance of getting out of its way. Fortunately, its interest in me was mere curiosity and, with that satisfied, it turned away and resumed its journey to the other side. I pondered the wisdom of my project for a moment and then went back to the job of building a hide on stilts to photograph the Little Kingfisher that came there each day.

Above: John Young building a hide on stilts to photograph Little Kingfishers. Opposite bottom: The set-up for bird-activated photography at the nest, triggered by an infra-red beam. The beam comes from the small black box at top left and is reflected from a mirror that is out of the picture. There are three flashes.

Photographing Australia's kookaburras and kingfishers took me to many fascinating parts of the country: the red sand and spinifex of far-western Queensland, hot and arid but intensely beautiful; the far north of Cape York with its erratic weather and the constant threat of being trapped by rising waters; the mangrove swamps and tropical woodlands of coastal Queensland; the exquisite rivers of Victoria's East Gippsland.

With most of the species it was not too hard to find nests, provided I was there at the right time. That was the difficult part, however, for breeding seasons are often variable and in the more remote areas I had nobody to call on to help me with local knowledge. To drive for two days and then find I was a month too early or, worse, a week too late was intensely frustrating but unavoidable.

Basic nest photography was also relatively free of problems, for most kingfishers are not as shy, nor do they nest as high, as the owls and raptors I have worked with before. However, to show them at their best, they need to be portrayed in flight and this did pose a few problems.

The ideal in-flight picture needs the bird to be large in the frame, sharply in focus and to be taken with an exposure short enough to freeze any movement. Flash is obligatory and with a fast-moving subject the only way to achieve focus and framing is to know beforehand exactly where the bird will be at the moment when the camera fires. The human mind and hand are too slow to keep

Opposite top: The author crossing the bridge to enter a camouflaged hide in a forest lagoon. Opposite bottom: The author in the creek, looking for an Azure Kingfisher nest. Left: Looking for the Little Kingfisher. The author in a boat with camera.

up with this and one answer is to use an infra-red beam, set up across the expected flight path of the bird and wired to fire the camera when the beam is broken. This method is entirely predictable, it does not suffer from lapses of concentration and it even allows the camera to look after itself while the photographer goes away to do something else.

There are problems, of course. Predicting the bird's flight path is not an exact science and there is also a delay between the breaking of the beam and the firing of the camera. This varies from camera to camera but may be anything from a tenth to a quarter of a second, time for the bird to pass right through the frame and out the other side. This distance has to be allowed for but there is plenty of room for error and I rarely got all the settings right first time. Inevitably, there were equipment failures and other frustrations but they faded away when everything fell into place and I found myself with an image that in life passed too quickly for the eye to grasp.

It is fortunate that most kingfishers are tolerant birds. There were times when I had the camera and three flash units plus the infra-red unit and its mirror, all clustered within a metre of the birds' expected course. As long as these were all introduced slowly, I never had any problems and it rarely took more than two bursts of flash before the birds began to ignore it completely.

I would have liked to include pictures taken inside a nest hollow and ones of kingfishers in the underwater part of their dives. The former is certainly possible but it involves a lot of human interference around the nest and I finally decided against it. As to the underwater dives, I tried for a year without success and finally had to admit defeat.

LOCALITY MAP

Timor Sea

Melville Island
Bathurst Island
DARWIN

INDIAN OCEAN

Litchfield N.P.
Kakad... N.P.
Nitmiluk (Katherine Gorg... N.P.
Keep River N.P.
Victoria
Da...

Drysdale River N.P.

Kimberley Region

Lake Argyle

King Leopold Ranges

Purnululu (Bungle Bungle) N.P.

Gregory

Broome
Cable Beach

Geikie Gorge N.P.

Durack Range

Halls Creek

Fitzroy

Tanami Desert

Tenn...

Port Hedland
De Grey
Dampier
Millstream–Chichester N.P.

Great Sandy Desert

**NORTH...
TERRIT...**

Chichester Range

Pilbara

Hamersley Range

Rudall River N.P.

Lake Mackay

West MacDonn... N.P.
Ali...

Cape Range N.P.

Karijini N.P.

Ashburton

Newman

Lake Disappointment

Gibson Desert

MacDonne...

Lake Neale

Kings Canyo...

Kennedy Range

Little Sandy Desert

Petermann Ranges

Uluru–Katatjuta
Katatjuta
N.P.

Cha...

Carnarvon
Shark Bay
Dirk Hartog Island

WESTERN AUSTRALIA

Uluru (Ay...

Monkey Mia
Hamelin Pool

Mutchison

Zuytdorp Cliffs

Lake Carnegie

Great Victoria Desert

S...

Kalbarri N.P.
(Pinnacles)

Geraldton

Lake Barlee

Lake Moore

Nambung N.P. →

Kalgoorlie–Boulder

Nullarbor Plain

Nullarbor Reserve

Nullarbor N.P.

PERTH
Swan
Rottnest Island
Fremantle

Wave Rock

Norseman

Lake Cowan

Leeuwin–Naturaliste N.P.

Margaret River

Stirling Range N.P.

Stirling Range

Esperance

Cape Arid N.P.

Nullarbor Cliffs

Cape Le Grand N.P.

Fitzgerald River N.P.

Manjimup

Walpole–Nornalup N.P.

Great Australian Big...

SOUTHERN OCE...

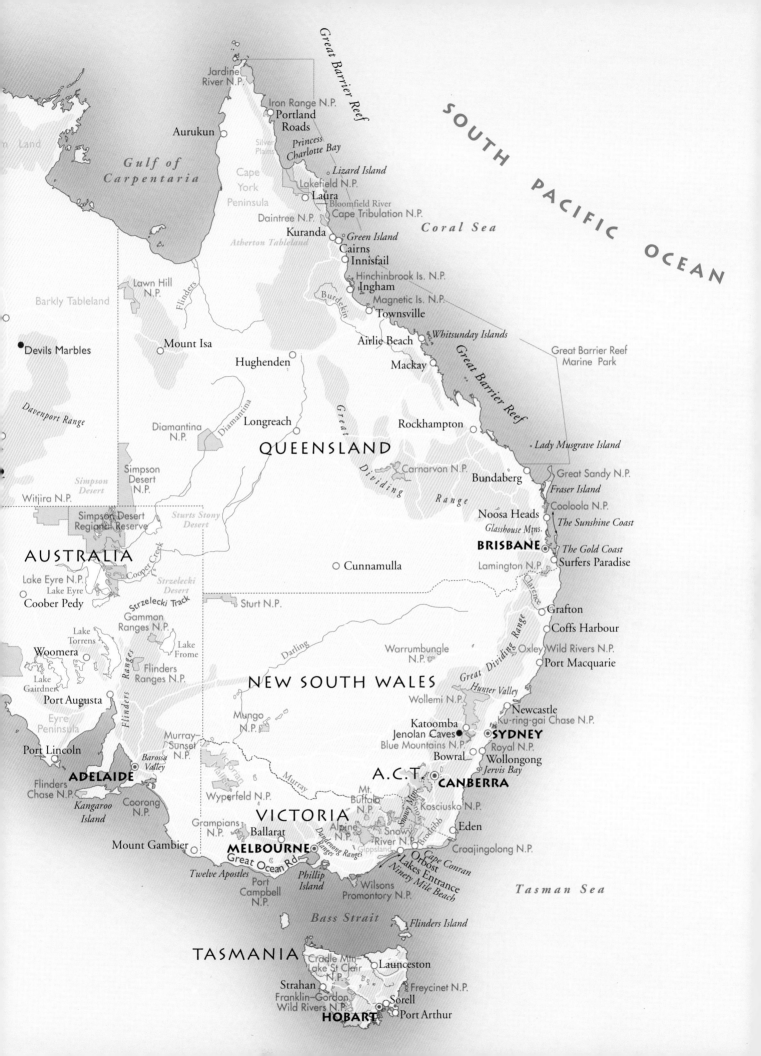

SOUTH PACIFIC OCEAN

Great Barrier Reef

Jardine
River N.P.
Iron Range N.P.
Portland
Roads
Aurukun
Silver
Plains
Princess
Charlotte Bay
Gulf of
Carpentaria
Cape
York
Peninsula
Lizard Island
Lakefield N.P.
Laura
Bloomfield River
Daintree N.P.
Cape Tribulation N.P.
Coral Sea
Kuranda
Atherton Tableland
Green Island
Cairns
Innisfail
Hinchinbrook Is. N.P.
Ingham
Magnetic Is. N.P.
Townsville
Lawn Hill
N.P.
Barkly Tableland
Flinders
Burdekin
Airlie Beach
Whitsunday Islands
Mackay
Great Barrier Reef
Marine Park
Devils Marbles
Mount Isa
Hughenden
Great Barrier Reef
Davenport Range
Longreach
Rockhampton
Great
Dividing
Range
Lady Musgrave Island
Diamantina
N.P.
Diamantina
QUEENSLAND
Carnarvon N.P.
Bundaberg
Great Sandy N.P.
Fraser Island
Simpson
Desert
Simpson
Desert N.P.
Cooloola N.P.
Witjira N.P.
Sturts Stony
Desert
Noosa Heads
The Sunshine Coast
Glasshouse Mtns.
Simpson Desert
Regional Reserve
BRISBANE
The Gold Coast
AUSTRALIA
Lamington N.P.
Surfers Paradise
Lake Eyre N.P.
Cooper Creek
Cunnamulla
Lake Eyre
Strzelecki
Desert
Clarence
Coober Pedy
Sturt N.P.
Grafton
Strzelecki Track
Gammon
Ranges N.P.
Lake
Frome
Coffs Harbour
Lake
Torrens
Oxley Wild Rivers N.P.
Port Macquarie
Woomera
Darling
Warrumbungle
N.P.
Great
Dividing
Range
Flinders
Ranges N.P.
Lake
Gairdner
Flinders
Ranges
NEW SOUTH WALES
Hunter Valley
Port Augusta
Wollemi N.P.
Newcastle
Eyre
Peninsula
Mungo
N.P.
Katoomba
Ku-ring-gai Chase N.P.
Jenolan Caves
SYDNEY
Murray–
Sunset N.P.
Blue Mountains N.P.
Royal N.P.
Port Lincoln
Bowral
Wollongong
Barossa
Valley
Murray
Jervis Bay
ADELAIDE
A.C.T.
CANBERRA
Flinders
Chase N.P.
Victoria
Wyperfeld N.P.
Mt.
Buffalo
N.P.
Kosciusko N.P.
Kangaroo
Island
Coorong
N.P.
Grampians
N.P.
Ballarat
Alpine
N.P.
Snowy
River N.P.
Snowy Mts.
Eden
Brodribb
Mount Gambier
VICTORIA
Dandenong Ranges
Snowy
Gippsland
Orbost
Cape Conran
Croajingolong N.P.
MELBOURNE
Great Ocean Rd.
Lakes Entrance
Tasman Sea
Twelve Apostles
Port
Campbell
N.P.
Phillip
Island
Wilsons
Promontory N.P.
Ninety Mile Beach
Bass Strait
Flinders Island
TASMANIA
Cradle Mtn–
Lake St Clair
N.P.
Launceston
Strahan
Freycinet N.P.
Franklin–Gordon
Wild Rivers N.P.
Sorell
HOBART
Port Arthur

FIELD GUIDE

AZURE KINGFISHER

Alcedo azurea (Latham, 1802)

Subspecies in Australia
A. a. azurea (Latham, 1802) Eastern and
SE Australia
A. a. diemenensis (Gould, 1846) Tasmania
only
A. a. ruficollaris (Bankier, 1841) Kimberley,
Top End and Cape York Peninsula,
N. Queensland
[Also subspecies in PNG, islands toward
Molluccas]

Other names Blue Kingfisher

Description A small aquatic kingfisher,
dark, glossy blue above and mainly
chestnut below. White nuchal blaze,
lores creamy white, throat white, bill
black with whitish tip, legs and feet red.
Northern birds tend to be brighter.
Australia's only other river kingfisher, the
Little, is much smaller, lighter blue above
and white below.
Length: 17–19 centimetres.

Voice A high, thin whistle, usually given
in flight but also when perched. Breeding
pairs often duet with briefer, staccato
versions of the whistle. The nestlings
call for long periods, making watery
swizzling sounds.

Food and hunting A fishing specialist.
Hunts from perches with a headlong
plunge into water, usually from heights
of less than two metres but sometimes
from considerably higher. Depth of dive
controlled by varying the openness of
the wings and the angle of entry.
Tends to have favourite hunting perches,
often in deep shade. Bobs head while
looking into water. Catches small fish,
crustaceans, tadpoles and, occasionally,
aquatic insects.

Breeding Season: In southern Australia,
September to February. About a month
later in the north. Victorian birds
frequently double brooded.

░░ *Race* Azurea*

▓▓ *Race Ruficollaris*

Display: High-speed chases, calling, by
two or three birds, just above the water.
Nest: A tunnel in a vertical bank, usually
over water but sometimes in a dry gully.
Tunnels horizontal or rising slightly,
45–70 centimetres long. Both birds dig,
tunnelling with the beak before emerging
backwards, kicking out the loose soil.
May use the same hole more than once.
Eggs: 4–7, white, round, glossy.
Incubation: About 21 days.
Young: Emerge pink, blind and naked.
Juvenile plumage like adult but bill
noticeably shorter.
Fledging: 28–31 days.
Post-fledging: Period of dependence
unknown but adults may lay a second
clutch within 10 days.

Habitat Creeks, rivers, lakes and
estuaries. Prefers those with ample shade
and overhanging trees.

Distribution Coastal northern, eastern
and southern Australia, including
Tasmania, from west Kimberley to the
border of Victoria and South Australia.

Distribution abroad Papua New Guinea
and the eastern islands of Indonesia.

*Race: a variety or subspecies.

LITTLE KINGFISHER

Alcedo pusilla (Temminck, 1836)

Subspecies in Australia

A. p. pusilla (Temminck, 1836) northern
Cape York Peninsula, Queensland
A. p. halli (Mathews, 1912) coastal Cairns
to about Townsville, E. Queensland
A. p. ramsayi (North, 1912) Top End,
Northern Territory, and SE Gulf of
Carpentaria, Queensland; rare in
between [Other subspecies from
Guadalcanal to Bismarck Archipelago
and New Guinea]

■ *Race Pusilla*

▨ *Race Halli*

▨ *Race Ramsayi*

Other names None known.

Description A tiny, aquatic kingfisher
barely one third the weight of the Azure.
Blue above, white below, with the blue
not as dark and glossy as in the Azure.

White nuchal patch and prominent white
lores, showing as two white "headlights"
in approaching bird. Bill black, legs and
feet black. Juveniles have crown faintly
barred, legs and feet pink.
Length: 11–12 centimetres.

Voice A shrill, thin whistle, very similar
to that of the Azure Kingfisher but even
weaker and higher. Inaudible to many
human ears.

Food and hunting Dives for fish and
small crustaceans in a similar way to the
Azure but rarely dives so deep. Diving
perch frequently only just above water.
Characteristically half opens and closes
wings while looking into the water,
possibly as a means of inducing fish to
move. Unlike the Azure, the Little also
hunts in forest canopy, where it takes
frogs, phasmids and other insects.

Breeding Little known.
Season: Wet season, particularly January.
Display: Unknown.
Nest: Said to use holes in banks like the
Azure Kingfisher but all nests known to
me have been in rotten logs and stumps
or in the base of epiphytic ferns. Tunnels
15 centimetres or less with small terminal
chamber. Most heights less than six
metres but possibly much higher.
Eggs: 4–5, small, white, rounded.
Incubation: Unknown.
Young: Unknown.
Fledging: Unknown.
Post-fledging: Unknown.

Habitat Streams, rivers, lakes, estuaries,
coastal mangroves, particularly
narrow, dark creeks in rainforest.

Distribution Coastal Northern Territory,
Cape York and north-east Queensland to
just south of Mackay.

Distribution abroad Coastal Papua New
Guinea and the Solomon Islands.

LAUGHING KOOKABURRA

Dacelo novaeguineae (Herman, 1783)
Endemic

Subspecies in Australia

D. n. novaeguineae (Herman, 1783) Eastern
Australia; introduced to SW of Western
Australia, Tasmania, Kangaroo and
Flinders islands; also to New Zealand
D. n. minor (Robinson, 1900) SE Gulf of
Carpentaria and Cape York Peninsula,
N. Queensland

▨ *Race Novaeguineae*

▨ *Race Minor*

■ *Introduced*

Other names Jackass, Laughing Jackass,
Great Brown Kingfisher, Ha-Ha Pigeon.

Description A very large brown and
white land-based kingfisher with a huge
bill. Head brown and white with crown

and broad stripe through eye, brown. Forehead streaked brown and white. Chin, throat and broad superciliary white. Nape white. Back and upper wings brown with pale blue mottling on wing coverts and large white patch at base of primaries, conspicuous in flight. Rump faintly mottled blue in mature males, brown in females and younger birds of both sexes. Upper tail rufous, narrowly barred black. Underparts and under wings white. Note that all the whites have a slightly "muddy" appearance. Bill massive, upper mandible blackish, lower dull yellow. Legs and feet pale flesh. Iris brown.
Length: 39–45 centimetres.
(A very familiar bird throughout eastern and south-western Australia, renowned for its raucous voice. Strongly territorial throughout the year with laughing choruses playing a large part in holding territories.)

Voice 1) A loud, prolonged series of chortles, shrieks and cackles, rising to a crescendo and gradually fading. Sometimes uttered singly but more often by up to five or, rarely, as many as seven birds, all shouting together in a discordant cacophony. Often answered in similar fashion by birds in adjacent territory. This "laughing" is the best-known call.
2) Alarm call: a deep, slow "Oo-waarr, oo-waarr" which may progress to the full laugh. Used also when coming towards the nest with food.
3) A chuckling flight call during the final approach to the nest.
4) Young in the nest call with constant hoarse rasps, becoming louder with age. These calls progress to hoarse shrieks after fledging but the full laughing call is not attained for many months.

Food and hunting A very versatile hunter taking a wide range of insects as well as larvae, arthropods, worms, frogs, skinks, snakes, mice and small birds, including nestlings. Most prey is taken on the ground by still hunting from a perch. Prey is seized with the bill after a glide and beaten against the perch. Occasionally dives for fish.

Breeding Both Australian species of kookaburra are cooperative breeders and the pair is assisted with incubation, nest defence and feeding the young by "helpers", usually between one and three.
Season: August to November.
Display: Slow, stiff-winged flights through territory by the pair, often in line ahead. Pairs perch together near prospective nest, particularly at dawn, arriving with low cooing call.
Nest: In southern Australia almost always in a hollow tree, usually the trunk. Heights from 2 to 30 metres. In northern Australia many birds dig hollows in arboreal termite nests. Very rarely holes in creek banks, walls or haystacks.
Eggs: 2–4, white, almost round, laid on a bed of woodchips or the bare floor of a termite mound. Clutches of more than three may be the result of two females laying.
Incubation: About 25 days. By whole group but mainly by the adult female.
Young: Emerge pink, blind and naked. Eyes open after a few days and blue feather quills appear. Feathers emerge directly from quills. Newly fledged young similar to adult female but slightly darker with shorter bills.
Fledging: About 28 days.
Post-fledging: Dependent on adults for about two months and may stay in family group after that.

Habitat In southern Australia: woodland, open forest, riverine forest, old gardens. In northern Australia, where it competes with Blue-winged Kookaburra: favours the denser and wetter forests, paperbark swamps and riverine rainforest.

Distribution Native to eastern Australia from Cape York to about Port Augusta and inland to about Longreach, Cunnamulla, the Darling system, all of Victoria and, in South Australia, the Flinders Ranges. Introduced to south-west Western Australia, Tasmania, Flinders and Kangaroo islands.

Distribution abroad An Australian endemic but introduced to New Zealand where small numbers survive.

BLUE-WINGED KOOKABURRA

Dacelo leachii (Vigors & Horsfield, 1827)

Subspecies in Australia
D. l. leachii (Vigors & Horsfield, 1827)
Kimberley, Top End and NE Australia
D. l. occidentalis (Gould, 1870) Pilbara area,
Western Australia
[Also subspecies in New Guinea]

/// Race Leachii

/// Race Occidentalis

Other names Barking Jackass,
Howling Jackass.

Description A very large, land-based
kingfisher with almost white head,
massive bill, prominent blue wing patch
and diagnostic white eye. All birds have
blue rump and adult males have whole of
upper tail blue. White head finely

streaked black, back brown, upper tail
rufous narrowly barred black, except in
adult males. Underparts whitish, faintly
barred brown, bill ivory.
Length: 40–46 centimetres.
(Confusion is possible only with the
Laughing Kookaburra. The Blue-winged
always appears much paler and more top-
heavy than the Laughing and is usually
considerably shyer.)

Voice 1) Family parties call in chorus
together as with the Laughing
Kookaburra but even louder and more
discordant. Usually starts with series of
explosive "Yok"s from one bird. Others
enter with strident howls, shrieks and
cackles, which may continue for nearly
half a minute. The chorus is frequently
answered by neighbouring birds.
2) A low, conversational "Ow" when
approaching the nest with food.
3) A harsh barking squawk when
suspicious.

Food and hunting Very similar to the
Laughing Kookaburra but the Blue-
winged appears to take a higher
proportion of snakes, possibly because
these are more common in the tropics.

Breeding A cooperative breeder like the
Laughing Kookaburra but occasional
broods are raised by parents alone.
Season: September to November.
Display: Few records but appears to be
similar to the Laughing Kookaburra.
Nest: In arboreal termite mound or tree
hollow. Strong preference for Poplar
Gum (*Eucalyptus alba*).
Eggs: Usually 2–3, white, almost round,
laid on bare floor of nest.
Incubation: Probably about 25 days.
Young, Fledging and Post-fledging:
All very similar to the Laughing
Kookaburra.

Habitat Primarily savanna woodland but
also timbered creeks, parks and gardens.

Distribution Coastal northern Australia
from the Pilbara in the west to just south
of Brisbane.

Distribution abroad Torres Strait and
southern New Guinea.

FOREST KINGFISHER

Todiramphus macleayii (Jardine & Selby, 1830)

Subspecies in Australia
T. m. macleayii (Jardine & Selby, 1830)
Cape York Peninsula and Eastern Australia
T. m. incinctus (Gould, 1838) Top End,
Northern Territory only
[Also subspecies in Papua New Guinea
and Aru Islands]

Race Macleayii

Race Incinctus

Other names Macleay's Kingfisher, Bush
Kingfisher.

Description A brilliant blue and white
kingfisher, the smallest of the dry-land
blue kingfishers. Forehead, crown, nape
deep violet. Prominent white patch on
lores, forming distinct "headlights" when
seen from the front. Back, rump, tail and
upper wings brilliant royal blue, flight
feathers darker with a greenish tinge to
the wing coverts. Prominent white patch
at the base of the primaries, visible only
in flight. Thick black line through eye
distinguishable from violet cap only in
very good light. Underparts pure white
with white extending onto hind neck,
usually forming a complete collar in
males but never in females. Bill black with
base of lower mandible paler. Legs and
feet grey-brown. Eye black.
Length: 18–23 centimetres.
(A very familiar bird in winter in northern
Australia where it perches on overhead
lines with White-breasted
Woodswallows.)

Voice 1) A high-pitched rattling trill,
descending slightly in pitch. Not unlike
the Yellow-billed Kingfisher but lower,
harsher and more rattling.
2) A short purring musical trill near
the nest.
3) A single harsh "Chack" when flying at
a mound to dig. Used also when flying at
other mounds in a distraction display. A
similar and comparable call to that used
by Collared and Sacred Kingfishers.

Food and hunting An extremely agile
kingfisher. As well as taking prey on the
ground in typical kingfisher fashion, the
Forest will chase and catch insects in, and
snatch prey from, the foliage of trees.
Takes skinks, very small snakes, spiders,
crickets, grasshoppers, moths and a considerable number of frogs, usually small
tree frogs. Occasionally dives for fish.

Breeding Season: August to December.
Display: Male trills from a prominent
perch and is joined on the same perch by
the female. They face each other with
wings half open, necks and bills
stretched upwards and call together with
excited rattling calls. This may be
followed by copulation.

Nest: Usually in an arboreal termite
mound but occasionally in a tree hollow
or earthen bank. Excavation begins with
one or both adults flying at the termite
mound from a perch a few metres away
and striking the mound with the bill.
When the outer casing of the mound is
breached, the birds cling to it and dig
with the bill.
Eggs: 3–6, white, almost round.
Incubation: About 18 days. In northern
latitudes, eggs frequently incubated only
at night.
Young: Similar to Sacred Kingfisher.
Fledging: About 25 days.
Post-fledging: Unknown.

Habitat In breeding season: open forest
and woodland, less commonly around
isolated waterholes, parks and gardens.
Outside breeding season: frequents more
open country, particularly canefields,
perching conspicuously on overhead wires.

Distribution Eastern and northern
Australia from just north of Newcastle
north to Cape York, the Northern
Territory and north-east Western
Australia. Summer visitor to south-east
Queensland and northern New South
Wales. Absent from eastern portion of
Carpentarian coast. Rarely more than
200 kilometres inland.

Distribution abroad Papua New Guinea.

RED-BACKED KINGFISHER

Todiramphus pyrrhopygia
(Gould, 1840) Endemic

Subspecies in Australia
T. pyrrhopygia (Gould, 1840) Australia
only (no subspecies)

Other names None known.

Red-backed Kingfisher

Description A medium-small kingfisher
with a streaky, erectile crown and red
rump. Forehead, crown white, finely
streaked black. Dark line through eye to
nape black. White collar. Upper back
and upper wings blue. Lower back and
rump rusty red. Upper tail blue.
Underparts white, except for black
axillaries. Bill and feet blackish. Female
slightly duller. Length: 20–24
centimetres.

Voice 1) A high, far-carrying, single
piping whistle, used mainly during the
breeding season when it is repeated
several times a minute for long periods.
2) A grating chatter when about to fly to
the nest.
3) A soft, wheezing whistle and a musical
trill, both used near the nest.
4) A frog-like single croak when about to
fly to the nest hole.
Young in nest tend to be silent.

Food and hunting Hunts from perches in
typical kingfisher manner, taking mainly
skinks. Also spiders, grasshoppers, other
ground insects and small snakes.

Breeding Season: September to February.
Most birds start in September and late
nests may be second attempts after failure
or, possibly, double broods.
Display: Unknown.
Nest: Mainly in cliffs, cuttings, creek
banks, washaways, quarries and old mine
shafts. Also recorded in termite mounds
and tree hollows. Both birds excavate,
often in extremely hard substrate. The
length of the tunnel can be from 40 to 50
centimetres, sloping gradually upwards
from the entrance. The Red-backed digs
a new tunnel each year and may return
annually to favoured sites (up to 14 holes
of varying ages were recorded on one
small section of old mine shaft).
Eggs: 4–5, white, rounded.
Incubation: About 20 days. Adults may
not incubate during day.
Young: Unknown.
Fledging: Between 21 and 25 days.
Post-fledging: Unknown.

Habitat In breeding season: deserts and
semi-deserts, dry watercourses, dry
woodlands. This is Australia's desert
kingfisher. Appears to have been aided
by human development, making nest
sites in road and rail cuttings, mine
shafts and quarries in areas where
suitable sites are naturally scarce.

Tendency to move to the coast in winter
where it frequently perches on power
and telephone wires.

Distribution Dry parts of mainland
Australia, excluding south-west Western
Australia, the most southerly parts of
South Australia and New South Wales
and most of Victoria. Absent Tasmania.

Distribution abroad An Australian
endemic.

SACRED KINGFISHER

Todiramphus sanctus (Vigors & Horsfield, 1827)

Subspecies in Australia

T. s. sanctus (Vigors & Horsfield, 1827) Australia; also Sumatra, Borneo, Philippines

T. s. norfolkiensis (Tristram, 1885) Norfolk Island only

T. s. vagans (Lesson, 1828) Lord Howe Island; also New Zealand and its adjacent islands

[Other subspecies New Caledonia]

Sacred Kingfisher

Other names Green Kingfisher, Tree Kingfisher.

Description A medium-small blue-green dry-land kingfisher. Male has forehead, crown, back greenish blue. Broad band through eye to nape black. Small loral patch creamy. Upper wings, rump and upper tail bright blue but never as blue as the Forest Kingfisher. Throat and upper breast white, extending back to form broad white collar. Rest of underparts cream. Bill black with horn-coloured base of lower mandible. Legs black. Female similar but duller.
Length: 20–23 centimetres.

Voice 1) A loud, far-carrying "Kik kik kik, Kik kik kik" repeated many times and used particularly by males at the start of the breeding season. Frequency diminishes as nesting progresses.
2) A harsh, drawn-out scream given by the female in response to the male and also probably by both sexes when arriving at the nest.
3) A low, musical trill when coming to the nest with food.
4) A short, staccato "Tac" used mainly when making flying assaults at prospective nest sites. Both Forest and Collared Kingfishers use a similar call.
5) A monotonous, rhythmic swizzling sound made by young in the nest.
(Outside breeding season the Sacred is usually silent.)

Food and hunting Takes a wide range of prey on the ground with typical kingfisher diving technique. Prey includes many insects as well as larvae, spiders, centipedes and skinks, less commonly frogs, small snakes, mice and nestling birds. Occasionally dives for fish.

Breeding Season: September to January in southern Australia, where it is often double brooded. Farther north a little later and single brooded.
Display: Unknown.
Nest: In Western Australia and southern Australia, almost always in tree hollow, usually a knot hole in the main trunk. Farther east, many in earthen banks, while most northern birds use arboreal termite mounds.
Eggs: 3–6, white, round.
Incubation: Mostly by female, about 18 days.
Young: Emerge pink and naked but grow rapidly to fill nest hollow. Bark below nest entrance becomes thickly coated with flows of faecal whitewash, which also spatters ground below.
Fledging: About 25 days.
Post-fledging: Fed by parents at first but moves away after a few days, presumably alone.

Habitat Open forest and woodland, particularly near water, tree-lined watercourses, parks, golf courses, mangroves.

Distribution Almost the whole of Australia where there is suitable habitat, including many offshore islands. Summer migrant to southern Australia as defined by a line running from just north of Brisbane to just north of Perth. Small numbers overwinter in the south. Casual to Bass Strait islands and Tasmania.

Distribution abroad Papua New Guinea, Indonesia, Solomon Islands, New Caledonia, New Zealand.

COLLARED KINGFISHER

Todiramphus chloris (Boddaert, 1783)

Subspecies in Australia
T. t. colcloughi (Mathews, 1916) coastal
E. Queensland and New South Wales
T. c. pilbara (Johnstone, 1983) Pilbara
region, Western Australia only
T. c. sordidus (Gould, 1842) Shark Bay,
Western Australia, coastal to
Hinchinbrook Island area, N. Queensland
[Other subspecies in Papua New Guinea
and many in Indo-Pacific region from the
Red Sea through India and South-East
Asia into the Pacific Ocean where occurs
on many islands]

Other names Mangrove Kingfisher.

Description A medium-large blue and
white kingfisher of mangroves with a
massive bill. Appears black and white in
poor light. Forehead, crown, back, rump
greenish. Upper wings greenish blue
with brighter blue primaries and
secondaries. Broad black line from base
of bill, through and below eye to nape.
Small white loral spot. Whole of
underparts white and white collar. Bill
long and heavy, black. Legs and feet
dark brown. Male slightly brighter
than female.
Length: 24–29 centimetres.
(Confusion is possible with the Sacred
Kingfisher but the Collared is
substantially larger, whiter below with a
proportionately longer and heavier bill.)

Voice 1) A loud, explosive "Kik kik, Kik
kik" used both as a territorial and an alarm
call is the most common call. Second
note slightly higher than first.
2) A short "Kakakak" and a soft trill when
approaching the nest.

Food and hunting Catches most of its
prey on the tidal mudflats within
mangrove forest. Takes mainly small
crabs but also other crustacea,
mudskippers and other small fish.

Breeding Season: August to March.
Frequently double brooded.
Display: Unknown.
Nest: Usually a hollow in an arboreal
termite mound but also uses tree hollows,
almost always in mangroves.
Eggs: 2–4, white, rounded.
Incubation: Unknown.
Young: Similar to Sacred Kingfisher.
Fledging: Unknown.
Post-fledging: May commence a
second clutch within two weeks of
young fledging.

Habitat In Australia, but not overseas,
exclusively a bird of the mangroves.

Distribution Along the coastlines of
northern Australia from Shark Bay in

Western Australia to the Clarence River
in New South Wales.

Distribution abroad Very wide coastal
range from the Red Sea eastwards to
India, South-East Asia, Indonesia, Papua
New Guinea and Polynesia.

Race Colcloughi

Race Pilbara

Race Sordidus

YELLOW-BILLED KINGFISHER

Syma torotoro (Lesson, 1827)

Subspecies in Australia
S. t. flavirostris (Gould, 1850) Cape York Peninsula, N. Queensland
[Nominate and other subspecies in Papua New Guinea]

Other names Lesser Yellow-billed Kingfisher.

Yellow-billed Kingfisher

Description A striking yellow, green and blue kingfisher of northern Cape York. Male has whole of head, excepting nape, deep orange yellow. Two patches on nape black. Upper wings dark green. Back and upper tail blue. Chin and throat white. Underparts pale rufous-orange, darker on flanks and fading to white on belly and legs bright yellow. Eye black, size accentuated by narrow ring, black. Female similar but slightly duller and with black crown. Black patches on nape usually joined. Both sexes have erectile feathers on crown, more so in male.
Length: 18–21 centimetres.
(The Yellow-billed Kingfisher is unmistakable when seen but remarkably cryptic and more often heard.)

Voice 1) Main call is a piercing, descending trill, which has been likened to a blast on a referee's whistle. Given with bill raised and tail cocked. The call usually lasts about two seconds but breeding birds, particularly males, may give a series of calls of this length, followed by one lasting up to eight seconds. The female's call is slightly harsher and lower. Call sometimes preceded by high "Pip pip pip".
2) A harsh "Tak" or "Tak tak tak" before digging, approaching the nest or scolding. Sometimes this call becomes a rattling alarm call and may go on to the trill.
3) An explosive buzzing call when diving in nest defence.
4) Young in the nest call constantly with a soft "Chew chew chew chew" sound.

Food and hunting Similar to other land-based kingfishers: insects, spiders, skinks, geckos, small snakes. Appears to take more prey in the trees than the Forest and Sacred Kingfishers.

Breeding Season: Generally November to January but variable, depending on the start of the wet season.
Display: Unknown.
Nest: In arboreal termite mound.
Eggs: 3–4, white, rounded.
Incubation: Duration unknown. Eggs often left to incubate themselves, particularly during the day.

Young, Fledging and Post-fledging: Little known. Young leave nest with short tails and beaks.

Habitat Lowland and riverine rainforest, particularly at the forest edge and in small clearings.

Distribution Northern Cape York Peninsula from about Aurukun in the west to Princess Charlotte Bay in the east. Occasionally south to Daintree and Cairns.

Distribution abroad Papua New Guinea.

BUFF-BREASTED PARADISE-KINGFISHER

Tanysiptera sylvia (Gould, 1850)

Subspecies in Australia
T. s. sylvia (Gould, 1850) breeds
Cape York Peninsula; winters to Papua
New Guinea
[Other subspecies New Britain, Papua
New Guinea]

Other names White-tailed Kingfisher,
Long-tailed Kingfisher, Silver-tailed
Kingfisher, Tcherwal-Tcherwal
(Aboriginal—Bloomfield River district).

Buff-breasted Paradise- Kingfisher

Description An extravagantly gaudy
kingfisher of north Queensland
rainforests. The general impression is of
a large blue and apricot kingfisher with a
massive red bill and long white tail
streamers. Forehead, crown, upper
wings and outer tail feathers royal blue.
Black band through eye extending to
nape and upper back. Lower back, rump
and long central tail feathers white.
Underparts rich apricot. Bill and legs
orange-red. Sexes similar but breeding
females often distinguishable by bent or
broken central tail feathers. Juveniles
duller and browner with short central
tail feathers and black bill.
Length: 30–35 centimetres, including
tail streamers.
(Despite its garish plumage, this is a
very cryptic bird in its rainforest
habitat. Shy and most commonly seen
in flight when the white back and tail
streamers are by far the most
conspicuous feature.)

Voice 1) A pulsing call of "Tcherwill
tcherwill tcherwill tcherwill" used by
newly arrived migrants to advertise
territories. This is given less frequently as
breeding progresses but is the most
commonly heard call.
2) A soft trill when close to the nest. This
is a sign of uncertainty or anxiety.
3) An explosive scream, which is the full
alarm call, used in nest defence.
4) Nestlings call with a soft but constant
swizzling sound.

Food and hunting Catches prey with its
bill like other kingfishers, hunting both
on the ground and in foliage. Probably
never dives in water. Most prey is small:
phasmids, beetles, insect larvae, spiders,
skinks. One record of a small tortoise.

Breeding Season: Migrants arrive
mid-November to early December and
begin breeding at once.
Display: Low-level pursuit flights
through forest.
Nest: In terrestrial termite mound. Uses
only the small, black mounds (*Eutermes*
sp.) which are exclusive to rainforest.
May use the same mound repeatedly but
always has to dig a fresh tunnel as
termites fill in the previous year's hole.
Eggs: 3–4, white, almost round.
Incubation: Unknown.
Young: Unknown.
Fledging: About 25 days.
Post-fledging: Period of dependence
appears to be short. Adults return to
Papua New Guinea in late March and the
young follow about two weeks later.

Habitat Lowland rainforest.

Distribution A summer visitor to coastal
north-east Queensland from Cape York
to about Townsville.

Distribution abroad Eastern Papua New
Guinea and the Bismarck Archipelago.

REFERENCES

Barker, R.D. & Vestjens, W.J.M. *The Food of Australian Birds, Vol. 1, Non-Passerines*, Division of Wildlife and Ecology, C.S.I.R.O., East Melbourne, not dated [1989].
Technical volume. There are 7 ½ pp. on the kingfishers' foods.

Beruldson, Gordon *A Field Guide to Nests and Eggs of Australian Birds*, Rigby Publishers Ltd, Adelaide, 1980.

Blakers, M., Davies, S.J.J.F. & Reilly, P.N. *The Atlas of Australian Birds*, R.A.O.U. & Melbourne University .Press, Melbourne, 1984.
Kingfishers pp. 323–332; remains the only current general atlas.

Boag, D. *The Kingfisher*, Blandford, Dorset, 1982.

Christidis, L. & Boles, W.E. *The Taxonomy and Species of Birds of Australia and its Territories*, R.A.O.U. Monograph no. 2, Melbourne, 1994.
Contains current accepted taxonomic sequence and list of recommended English (common) names.

Clancey, P. *Kingfishers of Sub-Saharan Africa*, Jonathan Ball, Johannesburg, 1992.

Coates, Brian J. *The Birds of Papua New Guinea, Including the Bismark Archipelago and Bougainville*, vol. 1, Non-Passerines, Dove Publications Pty Ltd, Alderly, Queensland, 1985.

Curl, D. *The Call of Kakadu*, David Curl in Association with the BBC, 1990 [video].

Eastman, W. *The Life of the Kookaburra and other Kingfishers*, Angus & Robertson, Sydney, 1970.

Fioratti, P. *Kingfisher*, HarperCollins, London, 1992.

Forshaw, Joseph M. *Kingfishers and Related Birds, Alcedinidae—Ceryle to Cittura*, illustrated by William T. Cooper, Lansdowne Editions, Melbourne, Sydney, New York, London, 1983i.

Forshaw, Joseph M. *Kingfishers and Related Birds, Alcedinidae—Halcyon to Tanysiptera*, illustrated by William T. Cooper, Lansdowne Editions, Melbourne, Sydney, New York, London, 1983ii.

Forshaw, Joseph M. *Kingfishers and Related Birds, Todidae, Momotidae, Meropidae*, illustrated by William T. Cooper, Lansdowne Editions, a division of RPLA Pty Ltd, Melbourne, Sydney, New York, London, 1987.

Forshaw, J. M. *Kingfishers and Related Birds*, illustrated by William T. Cooper, Lansdowne Editions, GEO Productions, Chatswood, 1993.

Fry, C.H. "The evolutionary biology of kingfishers (Alcedinidae)", in *Living Bird*, vol. 18, pp.113–160, 1980.

Fry, C.H., Fry, K. & Harris, A. *Kingfishers, Bee-eaters and Rollers*, Christopher Helm, London, 1992.

Heather, Barrie D., & Robertson, Hugh A. *The Field Guide to the Birds of New Zealand*, illustrated by Derek Onley, 1st edition,

Viking, Penguin Books (NZ) Ltd, Albany, Auckland, New Zealand, 1996.

Heinsohn, R. "When Good Help Is Hard To Find", in *Nature Australia* Magazine, vol. 25, no. 8, 1997.

Higgins, P. & Davies, S.J.J.F. *Handbook of Australian, New Zealand and Antarctic Birds*, vol. IV, Parrots to Dollarbird, Oxford University Press, Melbourne, in press 1998.

Johnstone, R.E. "A review of the Mangrove Kingfisher, Halcyon chloris (Boddaert) in Australia, with a description of a new subspecies from Western Australia", in *Records of the W.A. Museum*, vol. 11, pp 25–31, 1983.

Parry, Veronica, *Kookaburras*, Lansdowne Press, Melbourne, 1970.

Pizzey, G. & Knight, F. *Field Guide to the Birds of Australia*, Angus & Robertson, Sydney, 1997.

Reyer, H.-V. & Schmidl, D. "Helpers have little to laugh about: group structure and vocalization in the Laughing kookaburra *Dacelo novaeguineae*", in *The Emu*, vol. 88, pp. 150–160, 1988.

Schodde, R. & Mason, I.J. "Aves (Columbidae to Coraciidae)", in Houston, W.W.K. & Wells, A. (eds) *Zoological Catalogue of Australia*, vol. 37.2, C.S.I.R.O. Publishing, Melbourne, 1997.

Schodde, Richard & Tidemann, Sonia C. (consultant eds) Reader's Digest *Complete Book of Australian Birds*, 2nd edition, Reader's Digest Services Pty Ltd (Inc. in NSW), Surry Hills, N.S.W., Australia, 1986.

Sibley, C.G. & Ahlquist, J.E. *Phylogeny and Classification of Birds: A Study in Molecular Evolution*, Yale University Press, New Haven, 1990.

Sibley, C.G. & Monroe, B.L. Jr *Distribution and Taxonomy of Birds of the World*, Yale University Press, New Haven, 1990.

Simpson, K. & Day, N. *Field Guide to the Birds of Australia*, 5th edition, Penguin Books, Ringwood, 1998.

Slater, P., Slater, P. & Slater, R. *The Slater Field Guide to Australian Birds*, Rigby, Sydney, 1986.

Strahan, R. (ed.) *Cuckoos, Nightbirds and Kingfishers of Australia*, Angus & Robertson, Sydney, 1994.

INDEX